PCs made easy

STAGE 6

easy

A PRACTICAL COURSE

Microsoft® Windows®

xp

edition

PCs made easy

STAGE 6

A PRACTICAL COURSE

Microsoft® Windows®
xp
edition

PUBLISHED BY THE READER'S DIGEST ASSOCIATION LIMITED
LONDON NEW YORK SYDNEY MONTREAL

PCS MADE EASY
MICROSOFT® WINDOWS® XP EDITION
A PRACTICAL COURSE – STAGE 6

Published by the Reader's Digest Association Limited, 2003

The Reader's Digest Association Limited
11 Westferry Circus, Canary Wharf, London E14 4HE
www.readersdigest.co.uk

We are committed to both the quality of our products and the service we provide to
our customers, so please feel free to contact us on 08705 113366, or via our Web site
at www.readersdigest.co.uk
If you have any comments about the content of our books, you can
contact us at gbeditorial@readersdigest.co.uk

®Reader's Digest, The Reader's Digest and the Pegasus logo are registered trademarks
of The Reader's Digest Association Inc, of Pleasantville, New York, USA

For Reader's Digest
Project Editor: Caroline Boucher
Art Editor: Julie Bennett

Reader's Digest General Books
Editorial Director: Cortina Butler
Art Director: Nick Clark
Series Editor: Christine Noble

PCs made easy – Microsoft® Windows® XP Edition was fully updated for
Reader's Digest by De Agostini UK Ltd from *PCs made easy*, a book series created and
produced for Reader's Digest by De Agostini from material originally published as the
Partwork *Computer Success Plus*
The new edition was adapted by Craft Plus Publishing Ltd

© 2003 De Agostini UK Ltd

Printed and bound in the EEC by Arvato, Iberia

ISBN 0 276 42757 2

CONTENTS

Windows

Managing user accounts

Once you have set up accounts for each person who uses a shared home PC, you will find that Windows' management tools can make sharing your PC with others more efficient.

Using Windows, you can set up individual accounts for each person who will share the computer. If you haven't already set up individual user accounts (see Stage 2, pages 18–19), do so now. It doesn't take long and, in addition to preserving your Windows settings, if you set up user accounts with passwords, it's the best way to keep your documents confidential.

Setting up user accounts can help to save time and effort for all users in a number of ways. For example, if you share your computer with other family members, you might find that your tastes in colours and icons on your Windows Desktop vary markedly. If another family member insists on using vivid reds and greens, but you prefer restrained greys and blues, you might find yourself endlessly swapping from one set-up to the other. The more people who share the computer, the more annoying and time-consuming this problem can become. Setting up individual user accounts solves this problem, as preferences such as Desktop settings, favourite file locations and so on are preserved for each user.

● Managing user accounts

Once you have created extra accounts for each of the people who share your PC, several handy tools become available to you. One of these is Fast User Switching, which is worth turning on straight away. Some families are reluctant to set up individual user accounts because of the additional time it takes when one person has to close the programs they are

using and log off to allow someone else to use the PC. Fast User Switching cuts this delay down to just a few moments, enabling users to get the best of both worlds – separate and secure accounts together with the ease and convenience of quick changeovers.

Other tools – such as disk space quotas – are useful for solving some of the problems that can arise when sharing your PC with others. Not surprisingly, even the largest hard disk can struggle to keep up with the demands of an entire family. If this happens, you can set disk quotas to keep things under control (see page 11). For example, setting quotas is a great way of encouraging any user who downloads lots of files from the Internet or who forgets to delete files that are no longer needed to become organized and disciplined in storing their files.

These tools are only available to users who were given Administrator status when their user accounts were originally created. The

idea is that the most computer-literate adults in the household should manage the PC, with children and others having Limited accounts to reduce the risk of major errors occurring.

● How Windows stores user accounts

For each account that an Administrator sets up on the computer, Windows creates a special set of folders. These folders are used for storing all that user's documents, but they can also store other useful information such as each person's Favourites menu and History

list – the list of recently viewed Web sites – in Internet Explorer.

Only an Administrator can manage user accounts, using the Control Panel's User Accounts program. For instance, deleting a user account removes the folders that Windows created to store that person's files. The Administrator is also given the choice of saving that person's files into a new folder on their own Desktop, or of simply deleting all of the files to free up disk space.

Limited user accounts

With a Limited account a user can view and change their own work but not that of other Limited users.

LIMITED ACCOUNT users have their own My Documents folder, visible only to that user and Administrators – but not to other Limited users. Sometimes it's useful to share a file with everyone, however. In this case, you can let anyone see and edit a file by adding it to the Shared Documents folder that appears in the My Computer window. Each user's email

account is kept entirely separate. This means that Limited users need not worry that others can see their email messages.

Although Limited users are restricted to accessing their own files and those that are shared, they can use the same tools for using and personalizing the PC as someone with an Administrator account.

Although an Administrator chooses the initial Start menu picture, a Limited user can change it to something of their own choice simply by clicking on it and selecting another picture (above).

Use the Shared Documents folder (left) if you want to store files so that other users can open and edit them without accessing your own account.

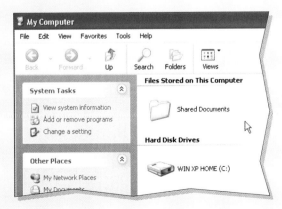

A Limited user can see only the Shared Documents Folder (left) in the My Computer window, whereas an Administrator can see this and all users' documents (right).

Using Fast User Switching

Windows can take a minute or more to log you off, which causes an annoying delay if another user needs to check their files quickly; the Fast User Switching facility cuts this wait to a few moments.

1 Most user account settings are made through the Control Panel. Select Control Panel from the Start menu and, when the main window appears, click on the User Accounts icon.

2 To make some useful changes that affect what happens when the computer is turned on or when different users want to log on, click on the 'Change the way users log on or off' link.

3 The next screen has two options. On most Windows XP computers, the first – Use the Welcome screen – is ticked. This option makes the Welcome screen appear when you switch on the computer. Although there are some minor security benefits to be gained from switching this off, it's best to leave this setting as it is.

4 However, the second setting – Use Fast User Switching – is potentially very useful in households where the PC is in constant use. Tick this box and then click on the Apply Options button.

5 This new option makes it much quicker for you to switch users on the PC temporarily. To use this option, the first person selects the Log Off entry in the Start menu. The Log Off Windows dialog box that pops up now has a Switch User button; click on this.

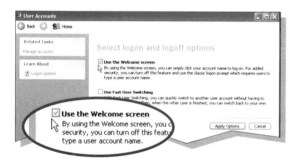

6 The Welcome screen appears, and the second person can now log on and use the computer. The beauty of this setting is that the first person doesn't need to save and close their files – Windows keeps them all in memory while the second person uses the computer.

7 When the second person has finished, they just click on Log Off again in the Start menu and then Switch User. The Welcome screen reappears, and the first person can then log back on and pick up exactly where they left off.

IMPROVING PERFORMANCE

If you're using the Fast User Switching feature, you may find that your computer slows down noticeably. This is because Windows uses up a lot of memory in storing your open programs and files, particularly if you use many programs at the same time that need a lot of memory. If you find the performance of your computer is affected, it's best to save your files and close all open programs before switching users.

Setting disk quotas

A family PC may come with a 40GB or bigger hard disk, but if you store many space-hungry files such as MP3s and digital photos, the hard disk may fill up quickly. Disk quotas can help you manage the space available.

1 To set disk quotas, you must have an Administrator account. Once you have logged on, open the My Computer window, right-click on the hard disk icon and select Properties.

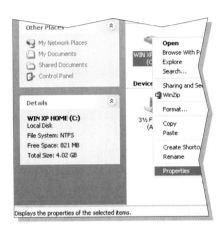

2 Click on the Quota tab on the Properties dialog box and tick both the 'Enable quota management' and 'Deny disk space to users exceeding quota limit' boxes. Then click on the Quota Entries button near the bottom of the dialog box.

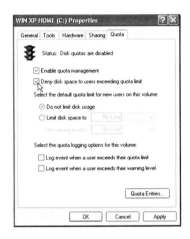

3 When the Quota Entries window appears, select New Quota Entry from the Quota menu. You now choose the first person you want to set a quota for. Type their name into the panel at the bottom of the Select Users dialog box and then click on the Check Names button.

4 Within a moment, the name you typed in is replaced by that user's full ID, prefixed by the name of the PC. Click on the OK button. Use the next dialog box to set a disk space quota. In this example, we've opted to limit the disk space to 10GB.

5 Set the warning level slightly lower and then click on the OK button to return to the Quota Entries window. This quota now appears at the top of the list. Repeat Steps 3 and 4 for other users of your PC.

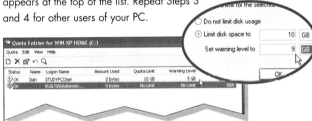

6 When you have finished setting quotas, close the Quota Entries window and click on the Apply button in the Properties window. Click on the OK button to start using your quotas.

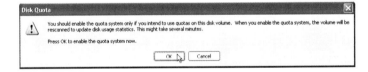

Make sure you explain the quotas and how they work to the people who share your PC. That way, they won't panic if they see the warning message boxes.

7 If any user exceeds the limits you've set, a message box appears. It prompts them to delete unwanted files to make the space they need.

PC TIPS

The space taken up by files in the Recycle Bin will also count towards the quota figure. It's therefore important to empty the Recycle Bin from time to time so that these discarded files don't stop you saving more important files.

Screen savers

Once a means of protecting your monitor from burned-in images, screen savers are now a source of fun.

Screen savers are special programs that monitor your use of Windows. When a screen saver notices that you haven't moved your mouse or pressed a key for a certain amount of time (for example, five minutes), it either makes the screen go blank or displays an animated sequence. The normal screen reappears as soon as you touch the mouse or press any key on the keyboard.

● Preventing burn-in

Screen savers were invented in the 1980s, at a time when monitors suffered from 'screen burn-in'. If static images were left on display for a long time, they would eventually leave a faint, permanent image on the screen itself. To avoid the problem, screen savers would detect when the computer was not being used and, after a short time, blank the screen. Although this prevented burn-in, the blank screen was a little dull and also made it difficult to tell whether the monitor and computer were on or off. Animated screen savers resolve these problems. They make it obvious that the computer is actually switched on and many screen savers are even quite absorbing to watch. Although an image is displayed, there's

Windows includes the familiar Flying Windows animated screen saver.

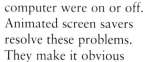

The following sites include a selection of free downloadable screen savers.

For a comprehensive list of thousands of downloadable screen savers, try FreeSaver at:
www.freesaver.com

At Screen Saver Heaven, you can choose from static previews of most available screen savers before you download them:
www.galttech.com/ssheaven.shtml

Drawing Hand is a unique screen saver that creates great works of art on your PC:
www.drawinghand.com/

no risk of screen burn-in, as the image moves and changes all the time.

Nowadays, you can download or buy screen savers that will display an array of weird and wacky animations. These can be anything from points of light appearing and disappearing to give you the impression of zooming through space, to a sequence of flying toasters or complex 3D animations – and even arcade-type games you can play with the keyboard. Indeed, some screen savers have become so engrossing that several companies have banned staff from using them!

● Greater choice

A selection of screen savers is supplied free with your copy of Windows XP, including Flying Windows, Blank Screen, Beziers, Starfield, Mystify and Marquee. Some of the screen savers can also be modified. The Marquee, for example, can take any short message you type in and scroll it across the screen.

If you would like to install a different screen saver, the two main sources are the Internet and commercial software packages. Internet downloads are often extremely

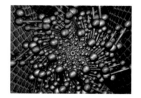

A flaming Desktop (top), Organic Art (centre) and sci-fi special effects (bottom) are just a few examples of the different types of screen saver you can choose for your computer.

high quality, and many are free. You can also find excellent screen savers based on TV shows or films, such as *Looney Tunes*, *The Simpsons* and *Star Trek: The Next Generation*, but these aren't free. Another popular screen saver is Organic Art. This features an almost limitless number of 'living' images, created by using complex artificial intelligence programs.

Starting your screen savers

Adjust your screen saver to make it go faster, slower or behave differently.

1 Screen savers are controlled from the Display Properties window. On the blank Desktop, right-click with the mouse and select Properties from the pop-up menu.

2 In the Display Properties window, select the Screen Saver tab. The screen that appears is split into two sections, with a large image of a monitor at the top. This shows a preview of the screen saver that is selected; it will be blank if you haven't set one up yet.

3 To pick a screen saver, click on the drop-down menu and choose one from the list. Depending on how Windows was set up on your computer, you might see different screen savers from those shown here (see Extra screen savers, right). Select the Flying Windows option. A preview of it will appear in the monitor box.

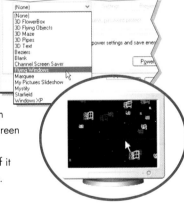

4 If you want to see how the screen saver looks on the whole screen, click on the Preview button. To exit the preview, simply move the mouse or press any key.

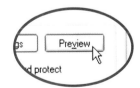

5 You can customize many screen savers. Click on the Settings button and a small window appears, allowing you to make changes. For Flying Windows, you can specify the speed of movement and the maximum number of 'windows' shown on screen at any time. Click on OK.

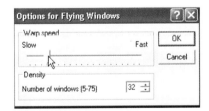

6 You can also specify how long Windows waits before starting up a screen saver. On the left-hand side of the Screen Saver screen is a Wait text box. Type in a number or use the arrows to change the setting.

7 Click on the OK button to return to your normal screen. The next time your mouse and keyboard are idle for the period of time you set in Step 6, your screen saver will appear.

Fine-tuning your PC's display

The Display Properties dialog box provides some useful ways of changing the way fonts, icons and windows are displayed on the screen.

The main methods of adjusting your screen are by choosing a screen resolution and a colour depth that suit the size of your monitor and provide the realism and detail you want to see in your documents and image files (see Stage 3, pages 12–13).

However, in addition to these fundamental settings, Windows also provides extra settings that you can alter and these will help you to get more out of your monitor.

● High resolution problems

If you have taken advantage of the big price reductions in monitors and have upgraded to a larger screen, you might find that the icons on the Desktop and in the folders seem too small. What happens is that when you change to a higher resolution (1280x1024, for example), the 32x32 pixel icons occupy a proportionately smaller area – less than a quarter of the area they would cover if the screen were running at a resolution of 640x480, for example.

By telling Windows that you want it to use larger icons on the Desktop and in folder windows, you can counteract this problem. It takes just a few moments to change, and if you don't like the effect you can switch back to the standard setting.

● Making text easier to read

Regardless of the resolution or size of your monitor, there are other ways to fine-tune your display settings. For example, when Windows displays text on the screen, it usually restricts itself to dots of just two colours – typically black on white – to form the characters as you type them. On many computer screens, this leads to a jagged effect where the curves and diagonals on the outlines of the letters take on a so-called sawtooth, or 'bitmapped', appearance.

Windows includes a little-known technology that can make text look a lot better (see PC Tips box, right). By filling in extra dots of colour between the jagged edges of the text and the background – such as grey dots for black text on a white background – the curves and outlines appear smoother. Not only does the text look better, but many people find it easier to read 'smoothed' text.

There is a slight downside to this process, however. Windows takes a small amount of time to add these extra dots to the information on the screen. On an old, low-power PC, you might find that scrolling around a 'smoothed' document seems to take quite a long time. If this is the case, you can simply turn the smoothing feature off and the problem will be eradicated immediately.

Smoothing fonts and increasing icon size

The Appearance tab of the Display Properties dialog box lets you tweak a number of useful Windows settings, enabling you to enhance the appearance and clarity of your on-screen work.

1 Right-click anywhere on the Windows Desktop and select Properties from the pop-up menu. When the Display Properties dialog box appears, click on the Appearance tab and then click on the Effects button.

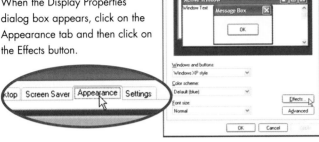

2 Tick the 'Use the following method to smooth edges of screen fonts' option. For now, leave the Standard method selected (see Smoothing methods box, below). Click on the OK button, and then on the Apply button.

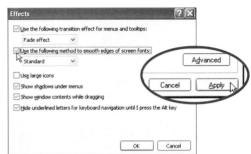

3 Now open WordPad from the Start menu's Accessories folder. Switch to a large typeface and type in some text. Notice that the curves and outlines of the letters are very smooth, with no jagged edges.

4 Switch back to the Display Properties dialog box. Remove the tick you just placed in Step 2, then click on the Apply button again. When you switch back to WordPad, minimize then maximize the window and take a close look at the more jagged letter outlines.

5 This is a close-up of a letter from each of the two windows. The extra grey dots in the image on the left will have a smoothing effect on screen.

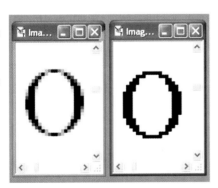

6 If you're using a high-resolution monitor, you might find the Desktop and folder icons appear too small, as on the Desktop shown right.

7 Switch back to the Display Properties dialog box and tick the Use large icons option. When you click on the Apply button, Windows redraws the Desktop and all the folders. The icons are now much larger, making them easier to double-click.

8 You might notice that some icons appear smoother and better drawn at these sizes than others. For example, the My Computer and Recycle Bin icons (below left) look fine, but the Creative Launcher shortcut (below right) looks blurred. This is because Microsoft created special large versions of its Desktop icons and stored them within Windows, but the Creative Launcher programmers didn't, so its large icon is just an enlarged version of the ordinary icon.

SMOOTHING METHODS

If you are using a desktop PC with a conventional monitor, select the Standard smoothing method (see Step 2) for screen fonts. If you are using a computer with an LCD panel, such as a notebook PC, select the ClearType option before clicking on the OK button. You won't do any harm if you select the wrong type, but you may find one more blurry than the other.

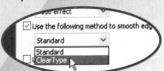

Recycle Bin settings

If you are fed up with being asked to confirm the deletion of every file or folder, you can change the way your computer's Recycle Bin works and save yourself time and irritation.

The Recycle Bin lets you recover items that you have thrown away if you later discover you needed them (see Stage 2, pages 20–21). Once you are familiar with its workings, and confident that you can recover files or folders after binning them, you might find Windows' frequent requests for confirmation of your actions (see Confirm action box, below right) irksome.

Windows does this as a safety measure to help teach PC novices to be careful about deleting. However, if it annoys you and you are aware of the dangers, you can tell Windows to delete files without the safety step (see opposite). The files will still be available if you need to recover them.

● Inside the Recycle Bin

The Recycle Bin icon is a shortcut to a folder that you don't usually see because it's hidden on the hard disk. When you delete files, they are removed from their original place on the hard disk and put in the Recycle Bin folder. Windows keeps a note of their original position. If you double-click on the Recycle Bin icon, the folder opens and displays the items you have deleted.

Windows generally uses up to 10 per cent of the hard disk space for the files you discard. Even on a small 4GB hard disk, discarded files take up a healthy 400MB. For most people, this is enough, but if you work with very large temporary files – video or audio files, for example – you might find it useful to increase the space available for the Recycle Bin. If you do this, the chances that anything you delete by accident will be available to restore later are increased.

Similarly, if you have a large hard disk – some new PCs have disks of 40GB or more – reducing the Bin's allocation to, say, three per cent still gives it 1.2GB maximum capacity while freeing up 2.8GB for files or programs.

The Recycle Bin acts like a real-life wastepaper basket. You throw things into it but can, if you want, retrieve them later. The Windows Bin has more tricks up its sleeve than an everyday rubbish bin, however.

CONFIRM ACTION

Whenever you press the [Delete] key after selecting a file or a folder, Windows asks you to confirm your action before you can proceed. A quick click on the Yes button does this, but over time this can amount to thousands of unnecessary mouse clicks which you may prefer to avoid.

Changing the Recycle Bin settings

If you find Windows' file deletion actions awkward or annoying, you can adjust the Recycle Bin settings to suit your individual needs.

1 Start by emptying your Recycle Bin so that the results of this exercise are easy to see: right-click on the Recycle Bin and choose Empty Recycle Bin from the pop-up menu. Click on the Yes button when Windows asks you to confirm your action.

2 Now right-click on the Recycle Bin again and select Properties from the pop-up menu.

PC TIPS

Deleting without a safety net

Think twice before ticking the Do not move files to the Recycle Bin option. If you then delete a file accidentally, your only chance of stopping the deletion is the confirmation dialog box. If you also untick the Display delete confirmation dialog option (see Step 3), to all intents and purposes, the Recycle Bin becomes less of a bin than a shredder. You will only be able to recover the deleted files with special utility software.

3 Under the Global tab of the Recycle Bin Properties dialog box, remove the tick next to the Display delete confirmation dialog option by clicking on it. Click on the OK button.

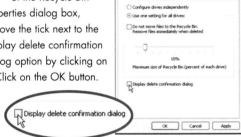

4 Create a test document in a program such as Notepad and save it on the Desktop. Close the document and then click on its icon once to select it. Press the [Delete] key on the keyboard.

5 The Recycle Bin icon changes to show that it contains something, but you're not asked to confirm your action. Double-click on the Recycle Bin to see the document. Restore it by clicking on the Restore all items link on the left.

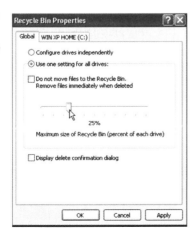

6 Your file is safely restored to the Desktop. Practise with other test files until you are confident about how the Recycle Bin now works. Note that the only time you are now asked to confirm any deletion action is when you choose the Empty Recycle Bin option (see Step 1).

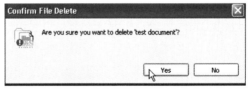

7 To change the maximum amount of hard disk space available for the Recycle Bin, repeat Step 2 to bring up the Recycle Bin Properties dialog box. Drag the slider to the right to increase the amount of space. On a 4GB drive, adjusting this setting to 25% gives 1GB of space for deleted files.

8 If your computer has two or more hard disks, you can select the Configure drives independently option if you want to try different settings for each hard disk. However, be aware that this may lead to confusion, with damaging consequences.

Accessibility options

A lot of work has gone into making computing easier for those with disabilities. Windows includes a host of accessibility aids that help make the software easier to use, several of which will be useful to all PC users.

Microsoft has a long history of developing accessibility aids. In 1988 it formally adopted accessibility development as a matter of policy, stating that it 'recognizes its responsibility to develop products and information technologies that are accessible and usable by all people, including those with disabilities'. It has lived up to its promises, today employing more than 40 people to work full-time in this area.

In 1988, Microsoft was asked by the University of Wisconsin-Madison to help make Windows 2.0 accessible to people with impaired dexterity and hearing. Over the years, this initiative has gained constant momentum, and each new Windows update has built further upon on the accessibility options of the one before.

● Assistive Technology

Microsoft has also made it much easier for third-party developers to integrate their own accessibility enhancements via what it calls Assistive Technology. This is a standardized approach to writing and providing software that is easy for disabled people to use. Most of the accessibility options available in Windows XP software build on the original Windows features, which include:
● The ability to change the size and colour of Windows elements (such as scroll bars, menu text and window titles) to help users with poor vision or colour blindness.
● On-screen captions instead of sounds (for applications that include a routine called ShowSounds) to help users with hearing impairment.
● Special keys to allow users with limited mobility to access various useful features: StickyKeys allow users who type with one

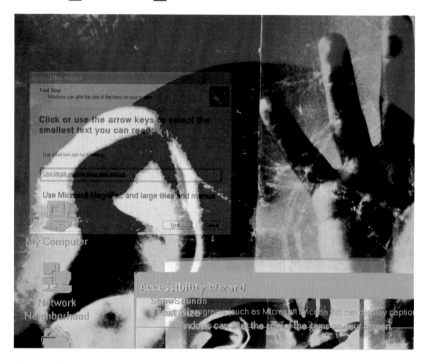

Microsoft offers a range of special features that provide easier access to the PC. These include software to magnify the screen, give a visual display of audible warnings and make keys behave in special ways.

finger or with a head- or mouth-stick to press two or more keys simultaneously; FilterKeys disregard keystrokes not held down for a specified length of time; ToggleKeys make the computer beep whenever the Caps Lock, Num Lock or Scroll Lock keys are pressed; SerialKeys let users control a PC using alternative or additional devices.

● Windows developments

As Microsoft has added more accessibility features to each version of Windows, it has also tried to make them easier to set up. The most useful outcome of this process is the Accessibility Wizard, which takes you step by step through the process of choosing between Windows' many different accessibility options. It displays all the options in one place, so you don't need to choose them through separate Control Panel screens. We show how to use the Wizard on page 20.

You can also customize individual aspects of many of the Windows settings, which can be particularly useful for the partially sighted (or even for those who have to wear reading glasses). The on-screen pointer, for example, can be displayed

PC TIPS

Options explained

It can be difficult to work out which accessibility options are most useful. If you want more information before starting up the Accessibility Wizard, read the explanations in the Windows Help file. First, select Help and Support in the Start menu, then click on the Accessibility link that appears on the left of the opening screen. The following page lists explanations arranged by topic.

in three different sizes and can be set to white or black, or to change colour in order to heighten the contrast with the background. The availability of more colour schemes means that Windows offers a greater variety of high-contrast options than ever before.

● A clearer view

One very practical utility is the Magnifier. As its name suggests, this allows you to zoom in (up to a factor of nine times) on an area selected by a mouse or keyboard. We show you how to use the Magnifier utility in the exercise on page 21.

The Magnifier can be extremely useful for all users, not just those who are visually impaired, because it offers an easy way of zooming in and out of the screen. This can be a valuable attribute, especially when you are dealing with particularly fiddly components, such as detailed graphics, for example.

CONTROL PANEL SETTINGS

In addition to using the Accessibility Wizard, you can specify accessibility requirements via the five tabs in the Accessibility Options dialog box, which is accessed via the Control Panel. For example, you can set the keyboard to avoid multiple keypresses. Or, if you have problems using the mouse, you can click Use MouseKeys under the Mouse tab to specify that you wish to press the numeric keypad to move the mouse up, down, right and left.

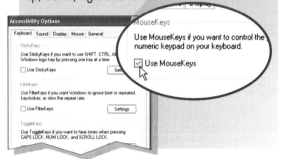

Other accessibility utilities

Windows includes several accessibility enhancements that you can try, but if none are suitable, you can go online to search for accessibility programs from other software developers.

THIRD-PARTY ACCESSIBILITY options are designed to benefit a wide range of users including individuals with poor or no vision; those who use a pointing device instead of a keyboard; anyone who talks to their computer rather than using a keyboard or mouse; and those who have difficulty with standard keyboards. For examples of the products listed here, as well as many other utilities, you can search a database on the Internet at: www.microsoft.com/enable/at/search.asp

Screen enlarger utilities

Also called large print products, these utilities allow the user to zoom in on a portion of the screen. This enlarged portion can then be moved to another area of the screen with the mouse or keyboard. Microsoft Magnifier, included with Windows (see page 21), is an example of this kind of utility.

Screen review utilities

Also called screen readers, these 'translate' the visual display, and present

it through alternative media, such as synthesized speech or a Braille display unit. Narrator is Windows XP's basic version of this type of program.

Voice input utilities

These allow you to control your computer, or input text, via the spoken word (see pages 116–117).

Keyboard enhancement utilities

These modify the behaviour of the Windows keyboard to make it easier for people with disabilities to use.

On-screen keyboard utilities

These utilities are designed for individuals with motion impairments, who cannot use a standard keyboard but might be able to point with a mouse or a headpointer, or to use one or more switches. The utilities present an on-screen 'keyboard' (which, in some cases, resembles an actual keyboard), offering choices that the user can select with a point-and-click or point-and-dwell interface. Windows includes a basic on-screen keyboard that

you can launch from the Start menu's Accessibility folder.

Miscellaneous utilities

This is a list of third-party developers of software (and a set of links to them) for those with various special needs.

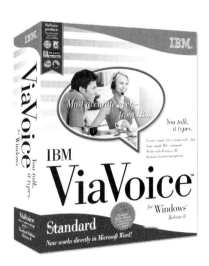

Voice recognition programs, such as ViaVoice from IBM, continue to improve in both their accuracy and their ability to transcribe at ever faster rates.

Using the Accessibility Wizard

The Accessibility Wizard allows you to configure Windows for your vision, hearing and mobility needs. Here we set a range of basic enhanced display options.

1 To start the Accessibility Wizard, select All Programs from the Start menu, then select Accessories, Accessibility, and finally Accessibility Wizard. In the first window, select Use large window titles and menus and click on Next.

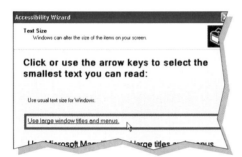

2 The next window offers a range of options for increasing text size. You might want to experiment with these to find the one that is most suitable for you. We have ticked Change the font size (we show you the Magnifier in action opposite). Tick the box and click on Next.

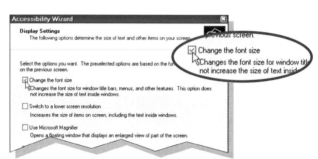

PC TIPS

Enlarge your screen
To quickly increase the size of all Windows elements, lower the screen resolution. To do this, select Display from the Control Panel. Then click on the Settings tab of the Display Properties dialog box and move the screen area slider all the way to the left. Click on OK. See Stage 3, pages 12–13 for how to change your display settings.

3 The next window allows you to specify what your vision, hearing and mobility needs are. Here we are going to set some options for those with vision and hearing difficulties. Tick the first two boxes and click on Next.

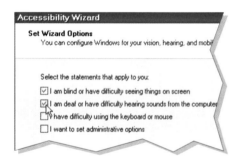

4 The next two windows let you specify the size of Windows' scroll bars and icons. Choose the size you want and click on Next each time.

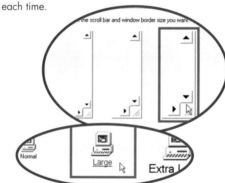

5 The next window allows you to select a high visibility colour scheme. Here, we've opted for High Contrast Black. Experiment if you wish – you can see the effects in the Preview panel. When you are happy with the display, click on Next.

6 The Wizard screen shows the new colour scheme and presents nine alternatives for the mouse pointer. Select one and click on Next. In the next screen you can alter the size and flash rate for the text cursor.

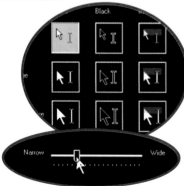

7 The next two screens set up on-screen notification of audible warnings. The first screen sets visual displays for system sounds (for example, a menu bar might flash, instead of a system beep). If you want this, click on Yes, then on Next. The second screen sets the system to display captions for speech and sound (this is only possible if it has been included in the application by the developer). Again, if you want this, click on Yes, then on Next.

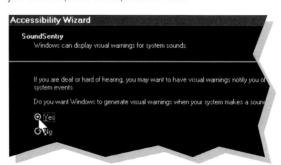

8 The final screen summarizes your changes. Click on the back button if you want to retrace your steps and change anything. Click on the Finish button to complete the Wizard.

Using Magnifier

The text produced by Magnifier is easier to read than ordinary sized type. Magnifier does this by behaving as if it were a real magnifying glass, enlarging just the area you want to look at.

1 To start the Magnifier, select All Programs on the Start menu and then Accessories. Choose Accessibility in the drop-down menu and then Magnifier.

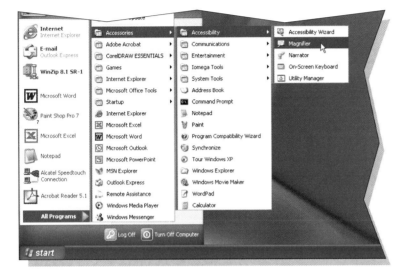

2 The Magnifier appears as a strip across the top of the screen. Use the Magnifier Settings dialog box to specify the Magnification level – we've increased ours to 3. As the tick boxes show, by default the Magnifier window takes as its focus whichever part of the screen is active – so it will either follow the cursor (whether controlled by the mouse or the keyboard), or text being typed into an application (see Step 4).

3 If you tick the Invert colors box, the magnification area at the top of the screen is easier to see. Click on the Minimize button on the Magnifier Settings dialog box.

4 To see the Magnifier in action, start up Microsoft Word and begin typing. Note how the Magnifier focus follows the text as you type it in.

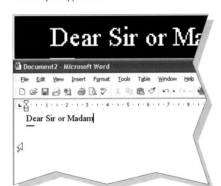

5 To turn off the Magnifier, click on its button on the Taskbar. In the Magnifier Settings dialog box, click on Exit. The screen now reverts to normal.

6 To undo all the accessibility modifications you made, restart the Accessibility Wizard and click on Next until you get to the screen that covers the setting you want to reverse. Choose the original settings and click on the Next button until you complete the Wizard and then on Finish.

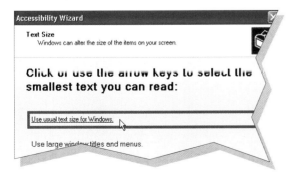

PC TIPS

Switching set-ups

If more than one person uses the computer, you might not want the same accessibility options constantly in operation. By far the easiest way to switch between normal and custom set-ups, such as those covered here, is to create different user accounts, so that there is one for each user (see Stage 2, pages 18–19). This saves a lot of time when you start your PC.

The Briefcase

If you need to move files between one computer and another, make sure that you never end up working on an out-of-date document by keeping important files in your Briefcase.

There are all sorts of occasions when it's useful to copy a file so that it can be worked on when you are using another computer. For example, if you own a notebook computer as well as a desktop PC, you might want to update files while on the move, or you might need to copy some urgent work onto a floppy so that you can finish it off on your home computer. And, if you help to run a club, you might find it useful to send some files to another member for updating.

In all such cases, there is a potential risk. As soon as a file exists in two places, it's possible for someone to update the wrong one. It is tricky enough to keep track of the most recent version, but if both get changed, the only way to sort out the mess could be to print them out and laboriously compare the two.

At best, this can be extremely annoying; at worst, it could lead to a costly mistake if a business ends up sending a customer an out-of-date price or an incorrect bill. Fortunately, Windows supplies a handy tool called the Briefcase to avoid this.

● What the Briefcase does

Windows' Briefcase acts as a special holder for important files that you can take with you from place to place. To save you having to remember which is the most up-to-date version when copying files, Briefcase controls the process automatically. It ensures that both the originals and the copies are correctly updated, without your having to move or copy them one by one. This automatic updating process is called synchronizing.

The Briefcase was mainly designed for use with notebook computers, so that if you use a notebook while you're on the move and a desktop PC at base, you can simply connect them and get Briefcase to synchronize whichever files have changed on either computer. However, you don't need to have a notebook to benefit, since the process works as well with copies on floppy disk. Briefcase only works with Windows – which means that if you are synchronizing files with someone else, they must have Windows, too.

● Automatic updating options

Briefcase automatically records any changes made, telling you which is the most recent version and letting you update any out-of-date files with a click of the mouse. For some files you can merge two versions of a document, both of which have been changed.

In Excel, for example, if you have altered cell B2 in one version and A3 in another, Briefcase can update the two files to reflect both changes. Beware, however, that not all types of file are merged this easily. It won't be as easy to work on a CorelDRAW image over two different PCs, and text files don't merge as well as Excel documents.

PC TIPS

Using a Briefcase to keep documents synchronized is very useful, but there are also times when you may want to stop this synchronization. For example, you might want to preserve the original form of a document that has since been updated on another PC. To do this, open the Briefcase file and select the file. Select Split from Original from the Briefcase menu and click the Yes button when Windows asks you to confirm your action.

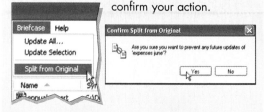

Using the Briefcase

Here's how to use the Briefcase to copy some important files to a floppy disk and keep track of any changes that have been made.

1 The first job is to create a Briefcase. You can create one in any folder. Right-click on a blank area within the folder window, select New from the pop-up menu and then select Briefcase.

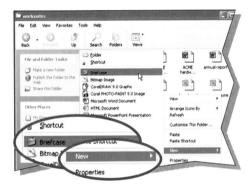

2 A New Briefcase icon appears in this folder. Select the files that you want to work on. Drag and drop them on to the new icon.

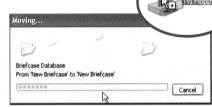

3 Put a disk in the floppy disk drive and open the My Computer window. Drag the New Briefcase icon on to the Floppy Disk icon. You'll see the normal Moving dialog box informing you of progress, and then the My Briefcase icon disappears, having been moved to the floppy disk.

4 Insert the floppy disk into another Windows PC, double-click on the floppy disk icon and you'll see the New Briefcase icon. Double-click on the icon.

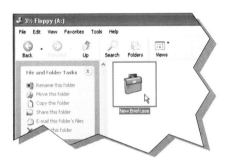

5 You can now see the documents that you copied in Step 3. The Status column on the right of the window reveals that both files are up to date. Let's assume you want to edit one of the files, so double–click on it.

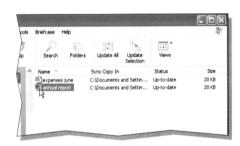

6 Make a few changes to the document and then save it.

7 Now take the floppy disk back to the original PC. Double-click on the floppy disk icon and then drag the New Briefcase icon back into the folder you used in Step 2.

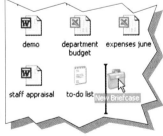

8 When you double-click on the New Briefcase icon, you'll be able to see the two files you have been carrying around. Notice how the Status column now reveals that the document we edited needs updating.

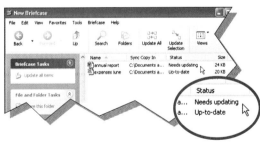

9 Select the edited document and then click on the Update Selection button on the window's toolbar.

10 Windows checks to see which version is the most up to date – the one in the Briefcase or the one on your hard disk. It then asks you to confirm the Update process. Check the details it shows you and click on the Update button. When the process is finished, both versions will include the changes you made in Step 6. Note that the information in the Status column now reflects the changes.

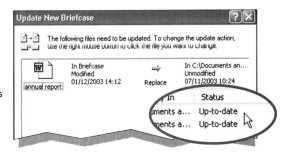

WordPad and Notepad

Two often-overlooked programs are installed by default by Windows. These are WordPad and Notepad, and they can be extremely useful when you want to do some quick and simple word processing.

Most new computers come supplied with professional word-processing software, very often Microsoft Word or Microsoft Works. However, Windows itself includes two word processors, and has done since the days of Windows 95: these are WordPad and Notepad. While neither of these programs can compete with Word in terms of features or options, they both have functions that make them useful for a surprising number of simple word processing tasks.

● Small but perfectly formed
Of the two, WordPad has the greater number of features and takes the appearance of a cut-down version of Word. It has many of the basic features of Word, such as simple formatting, text alignment and a few advanced paste functions. However, there are no options for tables or autoformatting, no borders or page breaks and no spell-checker. Despite this, you can write an ordinary letter or text document perfectly easily in WordPad and, if you need only simple formatting, it will look exactly the same as if you had created it in Word. WordPad documents even have the same .DOC file extension as Word. If you don't have Word or a similarly advanced word processor, then this is an obvious reason for using WordPad.

However, this program can also be useful even if you do have Word. This is because it is a much smaller program, so it is quicker to load and uses up far fewer system resources. This means it can be useful if you already have a number of other programs running at the same time. It is also handy for quickly loading documents for a brief look. Double-clicking on a file to load it in Word can take some time, but the same process in WordPad is almost instantaneous.

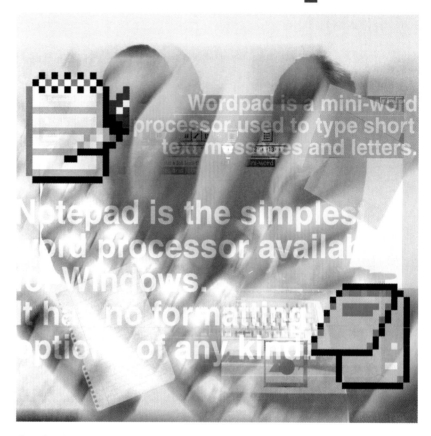

If you don't have Microsoft Word, you can get by with WordPad. Notepad is too basic for real word processing but also has its uses.

● The text and nothing but the text
At first glance, Notepad might seem much less useful than WordPad; it has no formatting options at all and barely any other options of any kind. But in the case of this program, it's a strength rather than a weakness. Owing to its lack of frills, Notepad is extremely quick to load and is perhaps the best program for browsing quickly through multiple documents. It is most commonly used to view text-based documents that do not have one of the familiar text file extensions.

Notepad is also useful for simple editing. For instance, if you know a few basic rules for writing HTML (see Stage 3, pages 132–133), you can use Wordpad to create simple Web pages. Although you can also do this with a complex word processor such as Word, you may want to avoid the additional formatting that Word can add. Notepad does not, and cannot, add anything other than text, so it is ideal for producing plain HTML, without any font or formatting commands.

WHAT IT MEANS

FILE EXTENSIONS

A file extension is a set of three or four characters added to a filename and separated from it by a full stop. Originally created in the days of MS-DOS, when the main operating system was text-only, the file extension gave the user an idea of the content of a file, as well as identifying the file type to the PC. Extensions are abbreviations, as in .TXT for Text, or acronyms, such as .GIF for Graphics Interchange Format.

Using WordPad and Notepad

Let's find out how these programs work and what features they have.

1 WordPad is accessed directly from the Accessories menu (inset, left) which is located in the All Programs folder on the Start menu. Word wrap – the automatic continuation of text from the end of one line to the beginning of the next – is enabled and different fonts can also be applied to specific sections of text by highlighting them with the mouse and selecting a typeface from the Font box.

2 You can also add simple formatting to the text. By highlighting text with the mouse you can add bold, italics, underlining or colour. You can also align paragraphs of text to the left, right or centre, and even add bullet points if you desire them. All these options are available from the Format toolbar.

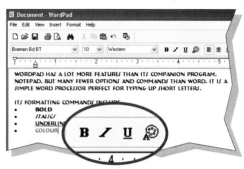

3 WordPad can also work closely with other Windows programs to create documents that combine text and graphics, for example. Select Object from WordPad's Insert menu and then choose Paintbrush Picture in the Object Type list. Click the OK button.

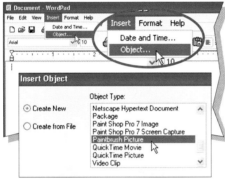

4 Now a painting area appears in the document. At the same time, the menus and buttons change to those of the Windows Paint program. When you finish your image, click outside the painting area to get the WordPad menus and buttons back.

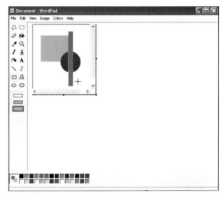

1 You can open Notepad, the simpler of the two programs, by clicking the Start button and selecting Notepad directly from the Accessories section of the All Programs folder.

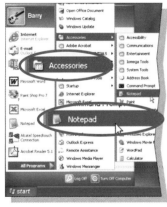

2 Notepad is extremely easy to use. Text typed in appears in the working document, as in Word or other large word processors. However, any text line that does not end in a carriage return (inserted when you press the [Enter] key), will continue along the same text row and disappear off your screen. To prevent this, select Word Wrap from the Format menu.

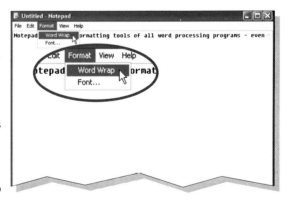

3 The Format menu's Font command lets you choose a typeface for the text in the Notepad window. Note that unlike WordPad and Word, you can't use several typefaces in the same document – your choice affects the whole document.

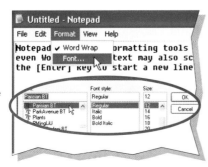

4 Most of NotePad's other menu commands focus on the file management and editing commands that are common to most programs, such as Open, Save, Print, Copy and Paste. If you want to timestamp your document, you can use the Time/Date command on the Edit menu.

Managing music with Windows Media Player

It doesn't take very long to build up a great library of MP3 files and copies of CD tracks, but if you're getting swamped by all the files you have, here's how to organize them.

The Windows Media Player program is the starting point for many of Windows' Multimedia activities. For example, it can play your music CDs, add an on-screen light show (Stage 4, pages 24–27), or tune into Internet radio stations (Stage 5, pages 138–141).

Besides this, it also has many features that aim to help you to get more from your music. For example, it can record tracks from your music CDs and store them on your hard disk so that you don't have to insert the music CD every time you want to listen to them. This makes it far more convenient to listen to music while you work.

● MP3 and WMA files
In addition to all these Multimedia features, Windows Media Player is also an excellent MP3 player. This means that you don't need to go to the trouble of obtaining a separate MP3 player program to listen to any MP3 music that you have downloaded from the Internet – you can simply use your existing Windows Media Player (see Playing MP3 files, opposite).

You may also come across some other types of Multimedia files on the Internet that automatically start up the Windows Media Player. For example, files saved in the Windows Media Audio format – which end in the .WMA file extension – are broadly similar to MP3 files and usually contain music. Windows Media Player can even play your WAV files (see Stage 5, pages 20–23).

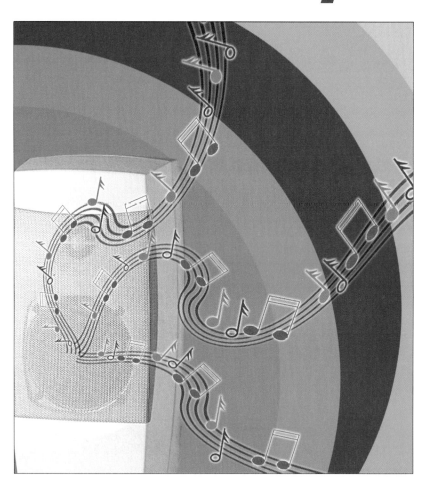

The Windows Media Player not only lets you listen to music: you can use it to organize your CD tracks, listen to the radio or play downloaded MP3s.

With all of these files and formats, you need some way of organizing them so that you can keep track of them and play them back without having to wade through folders full of files. By using the Media Library screen of the Windows Media Player, you can do just this.

● Keeping it all organized
With the Media Library screen, you can see all of your music files in one place. You can browse them easily and choose whichever one you want to play with a double-click.

WHAT IT MEANS

WINDOWS MEDIA AUDIO

Like an MP3 file, the music in a WMA file is stored in a compressed form so that it is quicker to download from the Internet. It was devised by Microsoft as a rival to the MP3 format, but is not yet as popular.

However, the real beauty of the program comes when you create your own playlists. Playlists are simply lists of the Multimedia files you have created, saved or downloaded. You can then use Media Player to create your own compilations and running order for your music files. For example, you could create a Dance playlist to use as the soundtrack for a party, or you could select a completely different set of tracks to create an Easy Listening playlist for use in the car.

On page 28, we show how to use the Media Library to help you keep track of your music and how to create and save playlists. Once you have made a playlist you'll then find out how to use it to produce your own compilation CD by following the steps in the exercise on page 29.

● Creating your own CDs

To turn a playlist into a CD, you need a CD writer drive in your PC. This operates in the same way as a CD-ROM drive, but it has the added ability of being able to use its laser to burn data onto special CD-R and CD-RW discs (see Stage 2, page 100–101). You can buy these discs from any retailer that sells software or office supplies.

You will also need space on your hard disk. Windows Media Player needs between 500MB and 1GB of hard disk space to create a data file called an image. This image is an exact copy of all the data that will be written to the blank CD. By storing it on the hard disk first, Windows aims to minimize the occurrence of problems that can stop or interfere with the CD-writing process.

Playing MP3 files

Windows Media Player lets you play back MP3 files that you have downloaded from the Internet, but on some PCs you may first need to tweak a setting.

● Using MP3 files

Windows Media Player can play MP3 music files. On most PCs, the program starts automatically if you click on an MP3 file on an Internet page, or if you double-click one that you have previously downloaded. You'll hear the MP3 music and see the same type of light show that you see when playing music CDs.

However, on some PCs you may find that a different program starts up when you double-click an MP3 file. Typically this happens if you have downloaded an MP3 player program, such as WinAmp. If you prefer, you can set up the Windows Media Player so that it plays back your MP3s instead.

To do this, start the Windows Media Player from the All Programs list on the Start menu and select Options from the Tools menu when the program window appears.

Select the File Types tab of the Options dialog box and place a tick in the MP3 Format Sound box (see below). Click on Apply and then on OK to make the change.

This icon indicates that another program – not the Windows Media Player – is set up to play MP3 files on this computer.

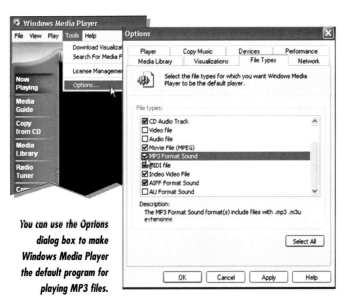

You can use the Options dialog box to make Windows Media Player the default program for playing MP3 files.

After tweaking the setting, the icon changes to indicate that a double-click on this file will automatically open Windows Media Player to play back the MP3 music.

Create a playlist

Make and save a sequence of your favourite music tracks so that the Windows Media Player can load and play the whole sequence whenever you want.

PC TIPS

Adding files to the Media Library

You may find that MP3s and other music files you downloaded from the Internet don't appear in the Media Library. To add them to the Media Library so that you can include them on your playlists, press the [F3] key while Windows Media Player is open. It scans your hard disk and adds all music files to the Media Library.

1 Launch the Windows Media Player by clicking on the Start button, then All Programs and then Windows Media Player. Click on the Media Library button when the Windows Media Player window appears.

2 Click on the New playlist button near the top of the window. A New Playlist dialog box pops up – type in a name for your playlist. Choose something that will help you to remember the type of music you are going to include on the playlist. Click on the OK button.

3 Your playlist appears as an entry in the My Playlists section in the panel on the left of the Windows Media Player window. Click on it once to select it, and the panel on the right shows that there are currently no music files in the list.

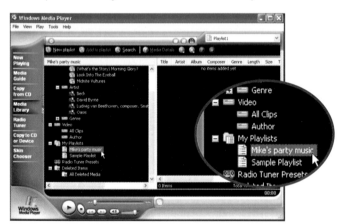

4 To add music tracks to your playlist, click on one of the albums listed in the panel on the left. The panel on the right lists the tracks from this album. Drag a track from this panel and drop it on to your playlist.

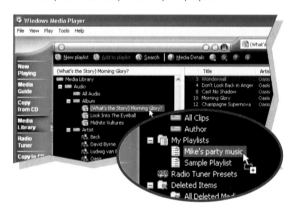

5 Repeat the process for other tracks you want on your playlist. You can review the tracks in your playlist at any time by selecting it in the panel on the left. If you change your mind about one of the tracks you have added, select it and click on the small 'x' button just above the playlist. Select Delete from Playlist from the drop-down menu.

6 You can use the up and down arrow buttons just to the right of the 'x' button to change the order of the tracks in the playlist. Each click moves the currently selected track forwards or backwards in the list.

7 Whenever you want to hear your playlist, all you have to do is select it from the panel on the left and then click on the Play button at the bottom of the window.

Turn a playlist into a compilation CD

If you want to listen to your favourite sequence of music files away from your PC, you can use Windows Media Player and a CD writer to create your own compilation CD.

1 Select your playlist in the Media Player. The first job is to check that the tracks are in exactly the order you want on the CD – you can't change them once the CD is burned.

2 Look at the line just below the list of tracks. This tells you how many tracks you have, and how much space they take up. If you have more space available (see PC Tips) you can add more tracks to the playlist to make better use of the CD.

3 Before you start to create your CD, close any other programs you have open to free up as many of the PC's resources as possible for the CD creation process. From the File menu, select Copy and then click on Copy to Audio CD.

4 The Windows Media Player switches to the Copy to CD or Device screen, which lists the tracks in your playlist. It also prompts you to insert a blank CD into your CD writer.

5 Once you have inserted the blank CD, a Ready to copy note appears in the Status column for each track. If you want to exclude a track from your compilation, remove the tick in its box in the listing.

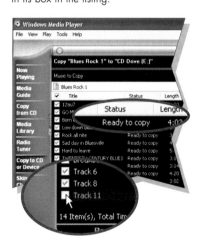

6 Click on the Copy Music button near the top right of the window. The first step in the process is the conversion of each track into CD audio data. You can monitor progress in the Status column.

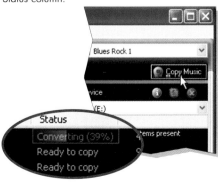

7 The second step is the copying of this data to the CD. The Status column keeps you informed of the progress – when the process is complete, the CD automatically pops out of the CD writer.

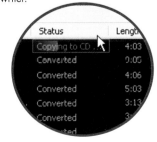

Software

Microsoft®Publisher

Outlining documents

Word's Outline function helps you to plan and structure lengthy documents in an organized way. It enables you to see the skeleton of your document at a glance and, if necessary, move entire chapters or sections in one go.

Single-page letters and other simple documents rarely require much planning, but if you have to create a document that runs to several pages or chapters, a lot more consideration has to be given to its structure. Lengthy essays and detailed business reports are normally broken down into distinct sections, which may be further sub-divided.

Word's Outline feature is invaluable when you need this kind of organized structure. As its name suggests, it is designed to help you set out a basic outline or skeleton, consisting of headings and sub-headings. You can then build up the detailed text. Outline also lets you apply a style to each heading, sub-heading and passage of text.

● Instant organization
The real advantage comes when you want to change the structure, as Outline makes it much easier to move whole sections around. You can collapse the document so that only the headings are visible, or you can expand it to view all the text. You can also move separate chunks of text by simply dragging and dropping headings into new positions.

If you have already created a large Word document it is still possible to use Outline's features. You can easily modify an existing

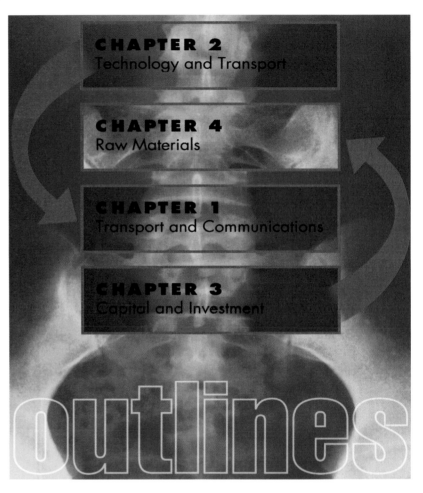

CHAPTER 2
Technology and Transport

CHAPTER 4
Raw Materials

CHAPTER 1
Transport and Communications

CHAPTER 3
Capital and Investment

document in Outline view, add headings and sub-headings, and move parts around.

Although Outline offers you a great deal of control over the organization of documents, it is no substitute for forward planning. The most efficient way to create a long document is to start with a pencil and paper and work out the separate sections and headings. You can then create a new Word document in Outline view and transfer your paper outline to the computer.

STYLES AND FORMATTING

You can apply a different style for the title, heading, sub-heading and text in your document using Word's Styles function (see Stage 2, pages 46–49). If you switch on Word's Styles and Formatting Task Pane, you can see a preview of each style and choose with a click.

New Document
Open ✓ New Document
Clipboard
Search
Insert Clip Art
New Styles and Formatting
Reveal Formatting
Mail Merge

PC TIPS

Show first line
When you collapse a document created using Outline, it shows only headings (bottom left). However, the bigger your document, the harder it can be to remember exactly what each part says. You can get a reminder of the content of each section by clicking on the Show First Line Only button (inset) on the right of the Outline toolbar. This collapses the document to its headings but includes the first line of text of each section (bottom right).

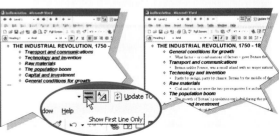

Using Outline with a long document

**In this exercise we show you how to use Outline to organize a lengthy document.
We've taken the example of a long history essay on the origins of the Industrial Revolution.**

1 Open a new Word document. Select Outline from the View menu.

2 A new Outlining toolbar appears under Word's normal toolbars, giving you all the options you need to structure your document. Type your main title at the top of the document and then a number of headings for the different parts, each one on a new line. You'll notice that Word selects the Heading 1 style for each of these headings; this is used for the top level of the hierarchical structure.

3 We want to make everything except the main title into a chapter heading. Select all the headings except the title and then choose Heading 2 from the Styles list box.

4 You'll now see that these lines have changed to the default Heading 2 style and that they have been indented, showing that they are below the title in the hierarchy of the document. You'll also see that the symbol at the beginning of the title line has changed from a minus to a plus sign. This shows that it contains a series of sub-sections.

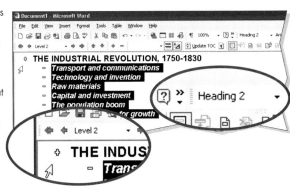

5 Now type in a few lines of text under the first sub-heading. Select this text and apply the Normal style from the Styles list box in the Task Pane. Add text in the same way for the other sub-headings.

6 To collapse the document to show only its outline structure – the headings – select all the text by pressing [Ctrl] + [A] and click once on the Collapse button (the minus sign on the Outlining toolbar).

The main text disappears, leaving only the bones of your document. The hidden text is represented by grey underscore lines, which appear under each heading.

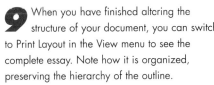

7 With your document collapsed, it's easy to re-structure it. If, for example, you think that the last section would be better placed immediately after the title, simply drag the plus sign next to its heading up the screen. Release the mouse button when the heading is in its new position. All the related text, represented by the grey line, has travelled with it.

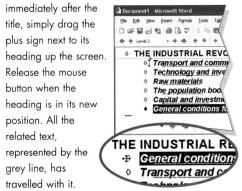

8 To view the complete document again, press [Ctrl] + [A] to select all the text and click on the Expand button (the plus sign on the Outlining toolbar).

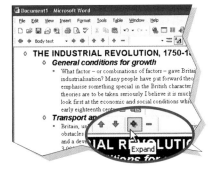

9 When you have finished altering the structure of your document, you can switch to Print Layout in the View menu to see the complete essay. Note how it is organized, preserving the hierarchy of the outline.

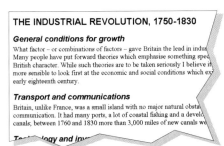

Page borders

An edging border holds the page together visually and can also help to convey its message clearly and effectively. You're not restricted to simple line-based borders, however. Word has plenty of formal and informal alternatives for you to experiment with.

Perhaps more than any other visual element, a page border helps to set the tone of a document. From a border comprising pictures of trees for a 'save the local park' leaflet to the fine and elegant lines used in a wedding invitation, a page border does more than simply enclose the text on a page. It focuses the reader's attention and draws the eye to the type of information the page contains. You don't need a special design program to produce competent page borders as Word will do the job for you.

We've already seen how to add borders to words and paragraphs within a document (see Stage 3, pages 42–45), but the best way to add a border around a page is to use Word's Page Border command. With a few clicks of the mouse you can try out hundreds of page border variations and then choose the one that suits the tone of your document.

● Types of border

Word offers a wide range of ready-made borders. The black-and-white, line-based borders are the simplest and they include multi-line variations that are perfect for formal documents. For less formal documents, there are many jazzy geometric borders: some are abstract, such as zigzag effects, while others have an Art Deco flavour.

If you want to use fun designs, Word also provides a selection of borders made up of pictures of palm trees, cake slices, musical notes and love hearts. Many of these are in colour, although Word allows you change the black in any black-and-white borders to another colour, thus increasing your design options even further.

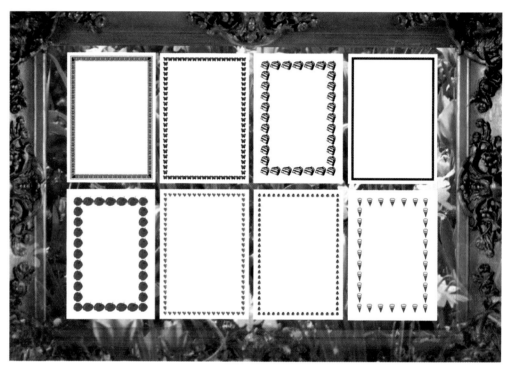

● Border alert

Borders are easy to add, but they can cause problems when it comes to printing. Some printers are unable to print close to the edge of the paper and this might affect one edge of the sheet more than the others. For example, inkjet printers can't usually print as close to the bottom as to the other edges.

If you find that one side of your border is missing from your printed page, change the margins (use the Options button in the dialog box shown in Step 2, opposite, to see the margin options). You may need to experiment to find the best settings.

Borders can enhance the content of your page. Experiment until you find one that suits the theme of your text.

WHEN NOT TO USE BORDERS

Page borders look great – but beware of going over the top. In many documents they can detract from the meaning and structure of your text. For example, as a border works to enclose an area of text, it's rarely appropriate to use an all-round border on documents where text runs from one page to another.

In cases where you would like to use the visual element of a border, you can tell Word to add a border only to certain edges of the page. For example, for a document where you want the reader's eye to be drawn from one page to the next, try using a border at only the top and bottom of each page.

Adding a page border

In this example, we'll use an appropriate page border to illustrate and jazz up a simple one-page menu for a restaurant that specializes in apple puddings.

1 Starting with a blank document in Word, select the Borders and Shading command from the drop-down Format menu.

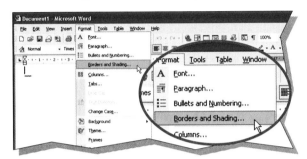

2 Click on the Page Border tab of the dialog box that appears and you'll see a screen with three main sections. The two sections on the left let you specify your border; the one on the right gives you a mini-preview of your page.

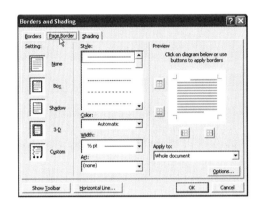

3 Scroll down the Style list in the centre of the dialog box and click on one of the multi-line options. You'll see the preview picture change to illustrate how your page will appear once the border has been applied.

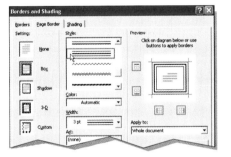

4 The multi-line border looks rather too formal for our menu, so click on the Art list box at the bottom of the dialog box. There is a huge selection of borders, so scroll down until you find one that looks right, and then click on the OK button.

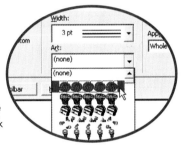

5 The border appears on the blank page. Only now can you see the size of the objects in the border. These apple pictures are a little too big, so bring up the Borders and Shading dialog box again and use the Width box to change the width of the border. Try a smaller value and click on the OK button again.

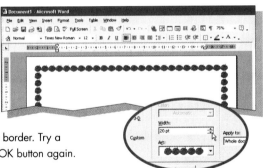

6 This page border is better for our purposes, as the apple pictures aren't so dominant.

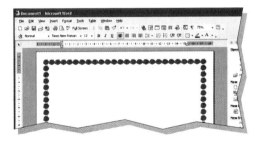

7 Check the Print Preview (see PC Tips box, right) so you can get the border position right from the start. Now it's simply a matter of adding the menu text and formatting it with your choice of typeface, size, colour and style.

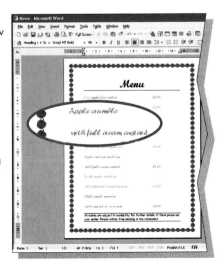

PC TIPS

Print preview
After adding a border to the page, but before printing your document, check the page with Word's Print Preview command (which is in the File menu). This last-minute check helps reduce paper wastage caused when one side of the border doesn't print out. This problem isn't revealed in Print Layout view and can only be checked in Print Preview.

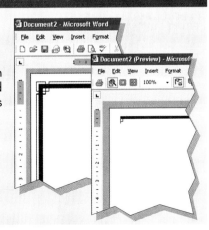

Using AutoText

Word's little-used AutoText feature fills in phrases from the first few letters you type. You can use its store of built-in phrases, or increase its usefulness by adding your own.

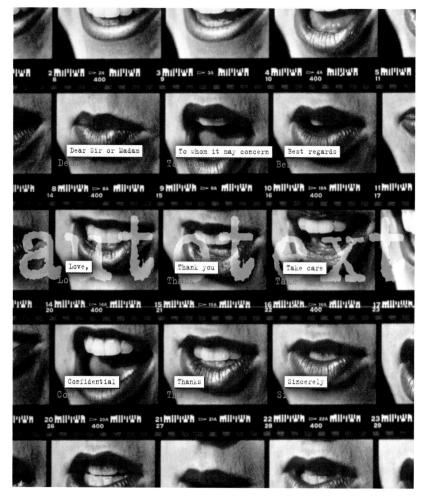

Word has many labour-saving features that are designed to reduce repetitive typing. AutoCorrect, for example, spots common typing errors or misspellings and corrects them (see Stage 2, pages 30–33). So if you mistakenly type 'teh' instead of 'the', AutoCorrect will fix it – often without you even noticing.

You can also use AutoCorrect to save yourself having to type out long phrases. For example, instruct AutoCorrect to replace 'RHS' with 'Richmond High School Parent and Teacher Association' and you'll save many keystrokes when it comes to writing an annual report or fund-raising proposal in which it is mentioned many times.

● Why use AutoText?

AutoText, while similar to AutoCorrect, has extra benefits. Perhaps the most important advantage is that instead of automatically making corrections, the AutoText function makes suggestions that you can take or leave as you see fit. You can see AutoText at work by typing the current month into a document.

AutoText in action: start typing 'Dear Sir or Madam' on a new line. Once you've typed a few letters, a small yellow text box pops up above your line. To accept the AutoText suggestion, press the [Enter] key and Word adds the rest of the phrase (left).

When you press the spacebar to insert a space after the month, you'll see a small yellow text box pop up above the letters suggesting that you add the full date. If you press the [Enter] key, Word will oblige by filling in the rest of the date, October 10, 2003, for example. However, this is only a suggestion; if you don't want to accept the AutoText insertion – if you only want to mention the month, say – just carry on typing and Word won't add anything.

● Odd suggestions

AutoText is one of Word's least-exploited features, mainly because it often seems to provide odd suggestions. For example, during the month of May, simply typing 'may' into any document will prompt Word to suggest AutoText for the date – May 21, for example. In addition, some AutoText entries use US English conventions. One of these is to have capitals on most words, as in 'To Whom It May Concern'.

Many people prefer to ignore AutoText suggestions altogether, rather than try to work out how they function. However, with a little effort, you can remove entries you don't use and add your own to make this feature more efficient. We show you how on the next page.

If you take the time to figure out how AutoText functions, you'll find it both efficient and timesaving.

PC TIPS

Be aware that AutoText can insert errors into your documents. If you want to start a new line of text while Word is suggesting an AutoText entry in a yellow pop-up box, pressing the [Enter] key will accept the suggestion rather than inserting a line break. If you insert a full stop (.) at the end of the line this will cancel AutoText's suggestion, but you should still use AutoText with caution.

Editing AutoText entries

If Word's existing AutoText entries don't quite fit your needs, you can change and add to them in seconds. Here's how.

1 Start a new document in Word and begin typing 'To whom it may concern'. Within a few keystrokes, Word suggests text to fill out the phrase. Unfortunately, it suggests US English capitals for all of the words.

2 To change this AutoText entry, click on the Insert menu, followed by the AutoText command from the AutoText sub-menu.

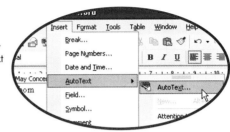

3 AutoText has its own tab in the AutoCorrect dialog box. Scroll down the list of entries until you can see the US version of the phrase. Click on it to highlight it and then press Delete.

4 Now you can add your version. Click on the text box above the list of AutoText entries and type: 'To whom it may concern'. Then click on the Add button and then on the OK button to return to your document.

5 Try typing the first few letters of the phrase again. Word now suggests your version; press the [Enter] key to accept this suggestion.

6 Adding new phrases is even easier. In this letter of complaint, we'll need to use the name 'Quiet-u-Vac', which is an awkward word to type often. Type it and select it. Click on the Insert menu, then on the AutoText item and select the New command.

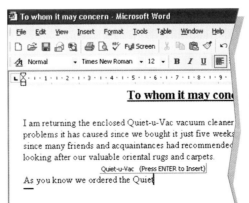

SHORT CUTS

Save time and effort when you want to create new AutoText entries by pressing [Alt]+[F3] once you have selected the word or phrase you want to add. Word will immediately bring up the Create AutoText dialog box (see Step 7).

7 The Create AutoText dialog box suggests a name for this entry (it does this because it will shorten very long phrases). You can change this if you want, but it won't affect the text that is actually added. Click on the OK button.

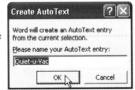

8 Now test the AutoText entry in the document. Type a few letters of the word (see Guessing with letters box, below left) and Word should suggest the full version.

GUESSING WITH LETTERS

Word's ability to suggest an AutoText word or phrase depends on the list of entries it contains – and how similar they are. For example, there are entries for 'Best regards' and 'Best wishes', but Word only knows which one you want when you type the sixth character – either 'r' or 'w'. Bear this in mind if you want to create several entries that begin in the same way. It might be quicker simply to key in the whole phrase yourself.

Adding power to your documents

Use Word's special OLE feature to add extra depth to your documents by making use of elements created in other software.

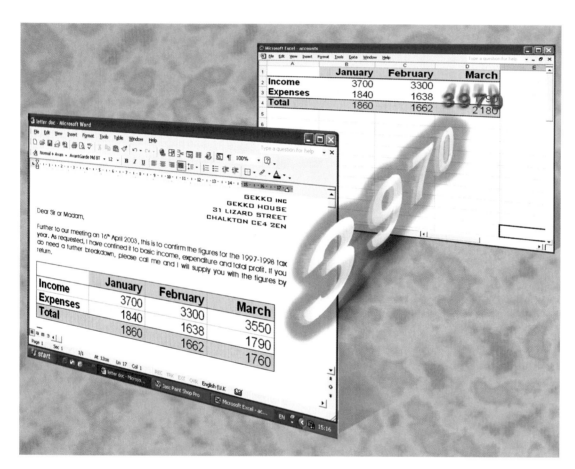

Windows' advanced OLE feature allows you to include a table created with Excel in a Word document such as a letter.

Through a number of Word exercises, we've seen that it's often useful to insert graphic elements from other programs into Word documents. For example, we've set up a document including a logo created in Paint (see Stage 1, page 49) and we've also seen how to import clip-art illustrations (see Stage 1, page 48).

So far, we've simply used these techniques to create documents that are more visually interesting. However, you can make Word much more powerful by including elements created in other types of program.

The key to this is to exploit a Windows feature called Object Linking and Embedding (OLE). Let's say, for example, that you want to write a letter including a table of figures – perhaps to support an application for a loan.

Word manages tables well, but it lacks the maths capabilities of programs such as Excel. By using OLE, you can insert an Excel table into your Word document. Even better, if you change the figures in your Excel table, Word can automatically pick up the changes so that its copy of the table is always up to date.

● Clever software
This powerful feature isn't restricted to Excel: it works with any OLE-compatible program, such as Paint, CorelDRAW or Corel PHOTO-PAINT. In fact, OLE is a blanket term for two similar ways of using programs together to achieve 'compound' documents. Once you get used to using these twin techniques of linking and embedding, you'll find that they open up new possibilities.

USE OF OLE

Although here we'll demonstrate how to use object linking and embedding within Microsoft Word, you can also use other programs in the same way. Both Excel (see Stage 5, pages 58–59) and CorelDRAW, for example, can accept OLE objects from other programs.

Microsoft® Word

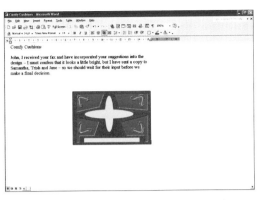

With a few clicks of the mouse it's easy to incorporate a design created in a graphics program into a letter. This is especially useful when using Word in conjunction with a graphic that will need several changes, as you can be sure it will be updated automatically.

OLE is really a feature of Windows rather than of individual software. Despite being somewhat under-used, it has been around for quite a while and is both widespread and reliable. If you are unsure about the OLE compatibility of any of your programs other than Word, check the documentation or look at the online help system. If they are compatible, they should work together, regardless of which company wrote them.

● Linking

The first OLE technique is linking. The example of incorporating an Excel table into a letter shows how linked files keep Word documents up to date automatically. You don't have to rely on your memory to ensure that the letter has the right data – Word uses Windows to check with the Excel worksheet.

This process could be particularly useful in situations where there are several people collaborating on one project. For example, an accountant could be working on some figures

HOW OLE WORKS

The object-linking process uses the Windows Clipboard just like other Copy and Paste operations (see Stage 1, pages 16–17). The subtle difference is that the Paste Special command gives you the option of linking the items you copy.

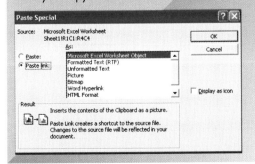

in an Excel table while a sales executive prepares the main part of the document in Word. Note that the information flow works only one way, from the source file (the Excel table) to the destination document (the Word letter). There can even be a number of destination files for a single source file (such as several different stationery designs linked to the same logo).

Another use of linking is to connect related documents for the purposes of cross-reference, or just to enable you to move easily from one document to another. For example, it's a simple process to copy a heading from one document and paste it into another as a hyperlink. Clicking on the hyperlink will then open the source document in much the same way as clicking on hyperlinks allows you to go from page to page when browsing the Internet.

● Embedding

Linking is only half of the OLE repertoire; the other half is object embedding. This impressive technique allows you to use the features and capabilities of one program while working in another (as long as you have both programs installed on your computer). For example, while using Word you can insert an Excel object. When you do this, the Word menus and toolbars will change to Excel's, and the Excel worksheet grid appears in your Word document.

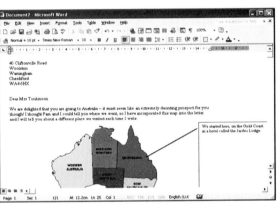

Embedding differs from linking because it does not require you to create separate Excel files. If we used embedding to incorporate an Excel table of figures, the numbers will be stored only inside the Word document. As a result, embedding is a quick way to set up compound documents using elements from other software. It's quicker than opening up other programs one by one and, as it doesn't create external files, it helps reduce clutter.

● Link or embed?

On the following pages, we demonstrate both techniques. As a rule, use linking when you already have objects created in other programs or when using the same object in several documents. Use embedding when working on one document and if you don't need its objects stored as individual files.

BRIEF WAIT

OLE is one of the most demanding tasks you can ask of Windows. You may therefore find that you have to wait a few moments for the screen to update when you carry out an OLE command. This is especially likely if you have a number of other programs open at the same time; this can cause Windows to move a lot of data around in order to open the various programs used in your linking and embedding projects.

You might imagine that it's just business users who can benefit from getting Word to keep track of changes to other documents. However, home users can apply the technique too. In the example above, linking is used to update a map in a letter giving a running report on a long tour.

Creating linked documents

Here we work through the process of linking documents. You'll find that it's quite easy to do and that it's a good way of exploiting some of the hidden powers of Windows.

IN THIS exercise we're going to create a letter that links two different files in two different programs, Word and Excel. Don't worry if you haven't got Excel; the part of the process demonstrating how OLE works is the same for other OLE-compatible programs. The basics of using OLE programs are covered in Stage 5, on page 58.

1 Create a new document in Word and then type and format a letter about some financial figures, for example a letter to the bank or to the tax office.

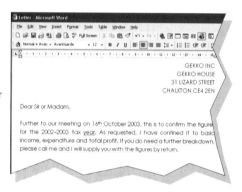

2 Without closing Word, open Excel. Click in the first cell (A1) and type in Income. Click in the next cell along (B1) and type 50000. Input the rest of the figures in the example in exactly the same way. We have put a formula in cell B3 (=B1-B2) to calculate the total.

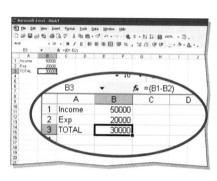

3 Use the mouse to select the cells containing your table. Select Copy from the Edit menu.

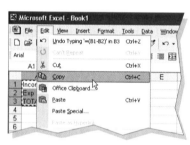

4 Return to Word and move the text-insertion point to the place where you want the figures to appear. From the Edit menu, select Paste Special.

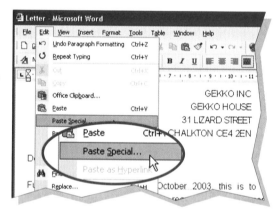

5 In the dialog box that appears, select the Paste link option on the left. Select Microsoft Excel Worksheet Object from the central list. Note that this entry depends on which application you are pasting the link from – if it is from Word, it will read Microsoft Word Document Object. Click on the OK button. The Excel cells will now appear as a table in your document (inset, far right).

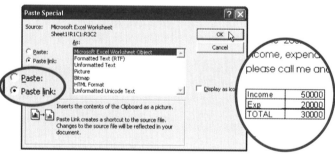

6 To see the power of linking the Excel table to the Word document, go back to Excel and change some of the figures in the table. We have increased the income by 10,000.

7 Now return again to your Word document and you will see that the figures in the mini-table have changed (inset) and now tally with your Excel changes.

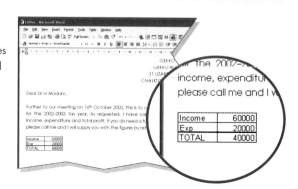

Embedding objects in Word documents

For this simple exercise that demonstrates embedding you will need another program to run within Word. We've chosen CorelDRAW, but the exercise will work with any OLE-compatible application.

1 Start a new document in Word and create a simple letterhead using Word's normal text formatting commands.

2 We want to include a graphic, which we can do by embedding an object from another program – in this case from CorelDRAW. Position the text insertion point below the letterhead, then click on the Insert menu and select the Object command.

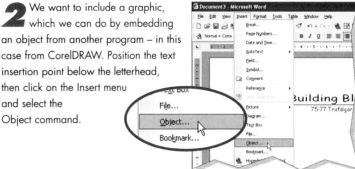

3 When the Object dialog box appears, make sure that the Create New tab is selected, then choose CorelDRAW 9.0 Graphic from the Object type list. Click on the OK button.

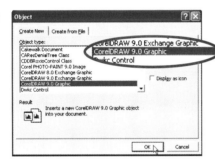

4 A few moments after the Object dialog box closes, a square drawing area appears in your Word document and you'll see Word's menus and toolbars have transformed into those of CorelDRAW (inset).

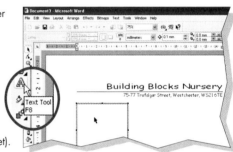

5 Use the CorelDRAW graphics tools to create a logo or picture in this drawing area. All of CorelDRAW's commands are available, so we've used shading options which Word lacks.

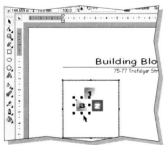

6 Click once outside the drawing area (inset) and the Word menus and toolbars will reappear with your picture in place below the heading text.

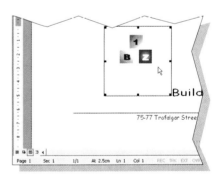

7 Click and drag the picture up to the top of your letterhead. When you release the picture, you'll see that it forces the text further down the page.

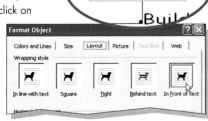

8 We don't want this, so click on the object with the right mouse button and select the Format Object command. Then click on the In front of text option under Wrapping style on the Layout tab of the dialog box.

9 Now you are free to position the picture object anywhere you want on the page without it affecting the text. This allows you to complete the logo on the letterhead, as shown.

Microsoft® Word

Indexing long documents

The longer your Word documents become, the harder it gets to find your way around them. If you add an index you'll be able to find any section of a document in seconds.

Long documents present their own special challenges. We've already seen how splitting them into sections makes handling multi-page documents easier (see Stage 5, pages 38–41). A writer can break a book up into chapters while a student's dissertations can be split into important sub-sections.

Long and unwieldy projects can become easier to use and appear more professional when they have an index.

● Automatic index generator
Such measures help make it easier to find your way around the document but, to make sure readers can find what they are looking for, the next step is creating an index. If you had to create it yourself, you'd probably never bother as it's a time-consuming task. However, Word has an automatic index generator. There are numerous kinds of indices available, including tables of contents, lists of references and much more.

● Indexing made easy
Creating an index in Word is essentially a two-stage process. First, you go through your document marking the words that you want indexed, then you get Word to build the index itself and insert it into your document. You can either index your document as you write it or after you have finished it.

If you want to index a document you've already written, you have a choice: you can either go through the document yourself or you can automate the process and get Word to help you out. The second method is less precise, but certainly less long-winded.

To do this, you create a new document that contains just the key words you need to index the work. Word uses this as a template to create the index on your long document. Word prepares the index by marking all occurrences of the key words automatically.

● Style selection
There are various different styles of index for you to choose from: Classic, Fancy, Modern, Bulleted, Simple or Formal. However, your choice might well be dictated by the style of the rest of the document. In addition, you can also specify the number of columns your index will have, whether you want your sub-indices to be indented or not and whether you want the page numbers to appear next to the index entry or be aligned on the right.

An index might take a little time to set up, but it will save you scrolling endlessly though a document to find the place you want.

PC TIPS

How the index works
As you go through the document and mark the words you want indexed, you'll see that Word places fields (see Stage 4, pages 38–41) next to them. These fields are for Word's reference only – they don't print out. To hide them from view, click on the Show/Hide button located on Word's toolbar.

Creating an index

For school work, business reports or hobby projects, an index helps you get the best from Word. We'll show you how.

Microsoft® Word

1 For this exercise, you'll need to create a multi-page document in Word – we've used a project about the Caribbean. Click on the Insert menu, then Reference, and then on Index and Tables from the drop-down list of commands.

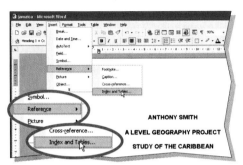

2 The Index and Tables dialog box then appears – this controls how your index will look. Leave the default format, From template, in the Formats box. For now we just want to tell Word which words and phrases to include in the index. Click on the Mark Entry button.

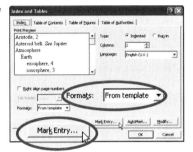

3 The Mark Index Entry dialog box appears. Scroll to the top of your document and find the first word you want to index. In our sample document it's Kingston. Use the mouse to select it.

PC TIPS

Updating your index

Your index can quickly become out of date, as Word can't keep track of any changes made. For example, if you add a title page to the indexed document, every page reference will be out by one page. Also, if you delete pages in the middle of your document, any words indexed later in the document will be wrong. To rebuild the index, right-click on the index and choose the Update Field option from the pop-up menu.

4 Now click back on the Mark Index Entry dialog box and you'll see the word or phrase appear in the Main entry box. Make sure the Current page option is selected in the Options section and click on the Mark button.

5 Word then adds a special field code to your document.

6 By clicking on the mark button instead of the Mark All button, we instructed Word to index just that particular mention of the word Kingston. Now we've selected another word, music. This time we want Word to include every mention of it in the index. Select it as before, but click on the Mark All button.

7 Mark other words in your document until you have done enough to create a good-sized index – for a general document two or three entries per page may well be sufficient. Click on the Close button and move the text insertion point to the place you want your index to appear – usually at the end of the document.

8 Bring up the Index and Tables dialog box again. Choose one of the formats from the drop-down list in the bottom left of the dialog box. Your chosen format will be displayed in Print Preview. Click on the OK button.

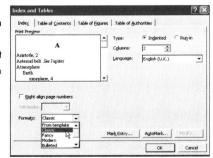

9 Here we've also selected the Right align page numbers option and a two-column layout with dots to take the reader's eye across to the correct numbers. Your selected words will automatically appear with their page numbers.

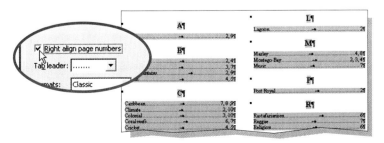

Advanced table design

To make the best-looking tables for your documents you have to look beyond Word's simple Table command. Instead, by using the Tables and Borders toolbar, you can create tables with much more impact.

In Stage 2, on pages 36–39, we showed how to add a table to your documents by using the Tables button on Word's Standard toolbar. Word then lets you choose how many rows and columns you want in your document, so it's easy to produce a convenient table to store information. This could be anything from a simple birthday list to a chart detailing financial transactions.

Word's tables work in a similar way to the worksheets that you create with Microsoft Excel. Starting from a simple grid, you can use table commands (see PC Tips box, right) to apply a coloured background to the individual rectangles – or cells – in your table. You can also combine cells to create irregular columns and/or rows. Word even allows you to carry out some simple calculations on the numbers in a table.

On the following pages you will find out how to create more complex tables by using

You'll be surprised at just how good Word's tables can look if you take a few moments to add colour and formatting to the basic text.

these extra features. You will also discover how simple it is to apply some additional formatting and so make a table much easier to understand.

● Creating complex tables

Although it is perfectly possible to build up a sophisticated table by adapting one of the simple tables created using the Table button, it is usually easier to use Word's Table and Borders toolbar. This brings together all the most important table commands and, since you can make the toolbar float on top of your document, it's much more convenient than repeatedly accessing the Table menu.

One of the main differences when using the toolbar is that in order to add a table to your documents, you simply draw the table in with the mouse pointer. In the same way, you also draw lines within the table to create its rows

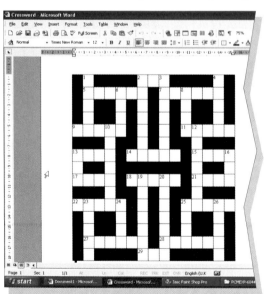

Tables created in Word can be very flexible. This crossword is simply a table with some numbers and black cell backgrounds added.

PC TIPS

Quick table commands

Whether you created the table by using the Table button or the floating Tables and Borders toolbar described on the following pages, you can get quick access to commands by clicking the right mouse button on the table. A pop-up menu (below) lists the common options.

PC TIPS

Inserting an Excel table

The simple AutoSum function described here will add up rows and columns of figures with no trouble. However, if your tables need to contain more advanced maths, try inserting an Excel worksheet. By using Windows' Object Linking and Embedding capability (see pages 38–41), you get the best of both worlds: tables with all the flexibility of Excel in a page with all the formatting features of Word.

and columns. The table and each of its cells can be resized with the mouse pointer. If you make a mistake, you simply use the Eraser tool to rub out the offending line. This makes it easy to create tables with irregular column widths and row heights.

● Table flexibility

There's also a great deal of flexibility in the way the table looks. You can colour and specify the weight (thickness) of borders. For emphasis, you can add colour to header cells and specific columns and you can even make every cell within the table a different colour. In fact, you can create some pleasing visual effects this way, which you could use to make a decorative feature or a logo, for example.

You can specify alignments in the table and within individual cells, and even run text sideways to create banner row headings. Rows and cells can be spaced automatically if, for example, you want to tidy up a table you have drawn yourself.

There is also a special tool called Table AutoFormat (see Using Table AutoFormat, below), which allows you to pick your design

from an extensive range of ready-made typeface and colour schemes. However, it's so easy to come up with your own schemes that you might well just want to use Table AutoFormat for suggestions.

● Maths calculations

When your table includes columns of figures, it's often useful to be able to add them up automatically. Word includes an AutoSum button, which works just like its counterpart in Microsoft Excel (see Stage 1, pages 62–63).

However, as you'll see in the exercises that follow, while Word uses its own internal guidelines to deduce which numbers you want to add up, it's always a good idea to check exactly which cells Word has added up when you use this tool.

AutoSum is just a simple, preset formula, so if you wish to perform tricky calculations, you can create more ambitious formulae in Word. However, you might find it's easier to do this in Excel. Alternatively, you can insert an Excel worksheet straight into your Word document (see PC Tips box, left) and so bypass the need to use a Word table.

Using Table AutoFormat

If you want to see just how much you can do to make your tables easier to read, browse through the ready-made schemes that are included with Word and which can be applied to your table instantly.

BY USING the Table AutoFormat command, you can try out many different formatting and colour schemes quickly. Word offers several combinations of colour, typeface and style, which you can browse through. Some of these are more suitable for informal documents, some are designed for black and white printers, and others are useful for presenting financial information clearly.

When you find one that you want to try, a simple button click instructs Word to apply the combination to your table. Even if none are exactly what you need, you might find one that is close enough so that you can apply it and then change just the few aspects that aren't quite right. This can be a lot quicker than starting from scratch.

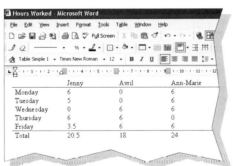
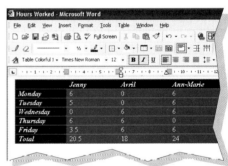

Here's the same table with four of Word's AutoFormat options applied. Some are simple and work well on any printer, but others are heavily coloured and will only work properly if they are printed using a colour inkjet printer.

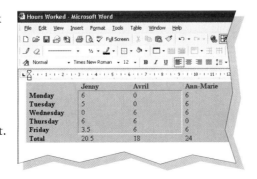

Drawing a complex table

For those occasions when you need a table with rows and columns of irregular height and width, it's best to use the Draw Table tool, as we show you here.

IF YOU insert a table into your document using Word's Table button, you'll find that Word assumes you want your table to have equal and regular column and row spacing. This, however, is rarely the case.

Often, you'll want the first or last row of your table to contain a title or heading that extends all the way across the table. While you can always tweak the regular table structure you get when you use the Table button, the drawing technique shown below enables you to create a table with exactly the right lengths and depths you need for the rows and columns in your table.

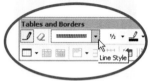
1 Start with a new, blank Word document and click on the View menu. Select Toolbars and then select Tables and Borders from the sub-menu.

2 The Tables and Borders toolbar will appear. If you have used it before, you might find that the toolbar appears at the top of your Word screen, under the existing toolbars. If so, drag it out onto the typing area of your document to make it float. Click on the Draw Table button at the far left of the toolbar, as shown below.

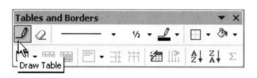

3 Use the Draw Table tool to draw the outer border of your table first. Click and hold down the left mouse button and drag the mouse pointer down and to the right to draw your table's outline.

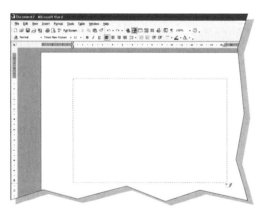

4 Still using the Draw Table tool, you can add lines to divide up rows and columns. Draw each one simply by dragging the mouse pointer from one edge to the opposite edge. Word automatically makes sure the lines are straight. Note that you don't have to draw all the lines to the outer edges; Word lets you start or finish at a dividing line you have already drawn (that's how we drew the single long cell that forms the first row). Don't worry if you make mistakes or if the spacing is uneven: you can tidy up all these problems later. Create a table that is similar to the one on the right so that you can follow the remaining steps.

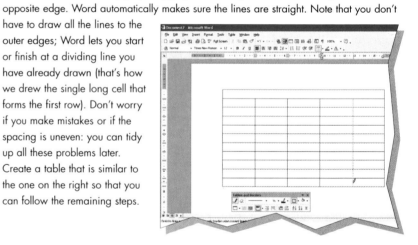

5 Now we will combine several cells into a single cell. First, click on the Eraser button near the left-hand end of the floating toolbar.

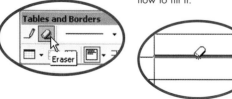

6 To erase a segment of any line, simply click on it. It will disappear and the two adjacent cells will be combined. Any text you type into this area will flow to fill it.

7 The table is now ready to have information typed into it. Here we have added some text to represent income and expenses for three executives in an office. Enter similar information into your table ready for the exercise on the next page.

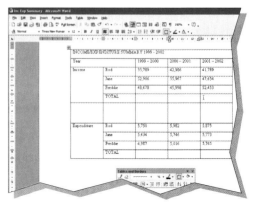

Advanced table formatting

The Tables and Borders toolbar has many single-click tools to help you create tables that are easier to read and more visually effective.

IN THE previous exercise, we created a table with cells of varying heights and widths. Other tools on the Tables and Borders toolbar can now be used for fine-tuning it: you can position text at the top or bottom of a cell, as well as aligning it to the left, right or centre.

You can also rotate an entry to run at right angles to the text. As you'll see in the example here, such techniques help to fit data into a table more efficiently. Other buttons control the style and colour for both text and background. AutoSum is also available.

Microsoft® Word

1 Start with the table you created in the exercise on the opposite page. Click on the multi-row cell that contains the word Income.

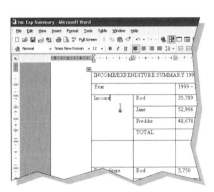

2 Now click twice on the Change Text Direction button on the Tables and Borders toolbar. The word will rotate to run at 90 degrees to its normal orientation. Do the same for the word Expenditure in the other multi-row cell.

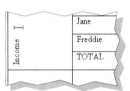

ROTATING TEXT

Each time you click on the Change Text Direction button, the text in the cell rotates clockwise. Note, however, that you cannot have upside-down text in a table, so there are only three possible orientations. Keep clicking on the button until your text has the orientation that suits your needs.

3 Click on the top cell – the one holding the title of your table. Then click on the arrow to the right of the Shading Color tool – this will cause the colour palette to open on top of your document. Click on one of the colours to select it.

4 The cell will change colour. Choose suitable colours for other important cells in your table. The aim is to make the information clear but not to make the colours so garish that the table is hard to read.

5 Now get Word to add up the figures in the table. Click in one of the blank total cells at the bottom of the table and then click on the AutoSum button. Word adds up the figures above and inserts the total. Word looks at the table and spots the blank line cell and, correctly in this case, assumes we don't want to include this in our calculations.

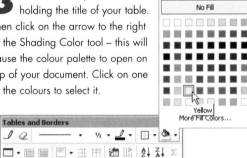

6 Use the AutoSum tool for the other total cells. Then select all the financial data in the table and use Word's Align Right button to make the data line up to the right of the cells. This helps make it easier to read, as the units, tens, hundreds and thousands align.

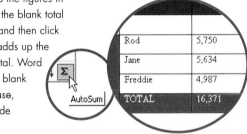

7 Some of the entries waste a lot of space, but if you need to change a row width or column height in your table, you can simply drag the borders with the mouse pointer. Make sure none of the tools are selected and you'll see that the shape of the mouse pointer changes as it passes over a border. Click and drag to move the border, as necessary.

8 Finally, select all the cells in the table and right-click on it; then select Table Properties from the pop-up menu. On the Cell tab of the dialog box, select the Center option. Finish off by using Word's standard formatting tools, such as the Bold button, to make the headings stand out.

INCOME/EXPENDITURE SUMMARY 1999 - 2002			
Year	1999 – 2000	2000 – 2001	2001 – 2002
Rod	35,789	42,986	41,789
Jane	52,906	55,967	47,654
Freddie	48,678	45,998	52,453
TOTAL	137,372	144,950	141,895
Rod	5,750	5,982	5,875
Jane	5,634	5,746	5,773
Freddie	4,987	5,016	5,765
TOTAL	16,371	16,744	17,413

Printing difficult documents

Printing A4 pages is straightforward, but Word also gives you the flexibility to print all sorts of other documents, such as greetings cards or invitations, in many different formats.

Most of the time, you will use your printer to print out pages on A4 paper. Apart from specifying in the Page Set-up and Print Properties dialog boxes that you are using this size of paper (and not the common default US Letter size), printing is usually a simple matter of calling up the Print dialog box and then clicking on the OK button.

However, there will be times when it's necessary to print out something different. You might want to print A5-sized pages for the Order of Service at a wedding, or perhaps a number of postcard-sized adverts to put in newsagents' windows.

It's perfectly possible to buy paper in many different sizes and most printers won't have a problem with any of them, as long as the sliding paper guide on the input tray can accommodate them and the correct size is set in the Print dialog box.

You have to be careful about paper weight, though. If the paper you use is too heavy or stiff, you could jam the printer. Check your printer manual for guidance.

● Trimming to size
Alternatively, you can print more than one page on a single sheet. For example, if you are printing an A5 Order of Service, you could print it 'two-up' (with the first and second pages of the document on a single sheet of paper orientated horizontally) then fold the page and perhaps bind it with a narrow, coloured ribbon.

Postcard-sized (A6) adverts could be printed four-up; simply cut them up afterwards using a guillotine or a craft knife and metal ruler. Always be very careful with the craft knife and make sure you have a suitable surface to cut on. A craft knife also comes in handy when you want to create a printed document with an element or picture that is positioned

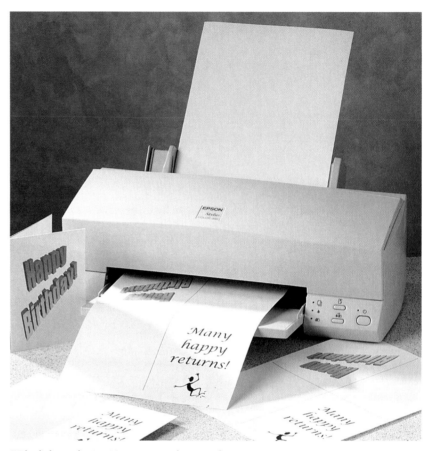

With a little pre-planning, it's easy to print documents that aren't a standard size, and fold or trim them to get the result you want.

flush to the edge of a page, as few printers can print right to the edge of the paper. In this case, you can trim the page, removing any unwanted margins. However, the page will then be smaller than A4.

● Controlling the printer
You can sometimes specify two-up or four-up printing by clicking on the Properties button on the Print dialog box. However, this is not always the case because the Print Properties are not a feature of Word, but of the printer and its software. Some printers have options that control settings which are specific to the printer. With a typical colour inkjet printer, for example, these options will usually concern colour and special paper options.

Don't worry if your printer doesn't offer any special printing options. Opposite we'll show you how to print special size and layout documents using Word. These techniques will work with any printer.

LABELS

You can buy sheets of labels mounted on backing paper for your printer but these only have to be a fraction out of line and the whole batch can be ruined. There are lots of variables that can cause problems, and therefore label manufacturers make labels in different shapes and sizes.

However, Word lists numerous types of label by product name, number and manufacturer. Try to restrict your choice of labels to these.

Creating a greetings card

Here's how to create a greetings card by printing on, and then folding, an A4 sheet.

Microsoft® Word

1 Open a new Word document and go to the View menu. Select the Drawing toolbar from the Toolbars submenu. On the floating Drawing toolbar, click on the Draw menu and select Grid.

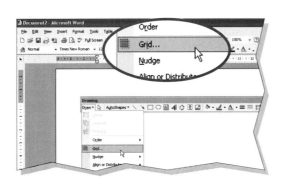

2 Tick the Snap objects to grid option. For Horizontal spacing specify 10.5cm, and for Vertical spacing 14.85cm (this is half the 21x29.7cm dimensions of A4). Click on OK.

3 Click on the Drawing toolbar's Text Box tool (inset). Word will switch to Page Layout view automatically. Click and drag to create four text boxes, putting one into each quarter of the A4 page. The grid makes them 'snap' to the correct proportions.

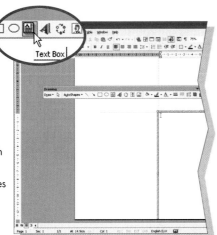

4 For the front of our card, we're going to add a WordArt greeting. Click the Insert WordArt button (inset) and the Gallery box appears. Select one of the styles and click on OK. In the Edit WordArt Text dialog box, type your greeting and then click on OK.

5 To position the WordArt accurately we need to turn off the grid. Bring up the Drawing Grid dialog box (as in Step 1). Make sure the Snap objects to grid check box is blank and then click on OK.

6 Now drag the WordArt greeting into the centre of the top-left quadrant. To make the card look right when it is folded we need to turn the WordArt upside down. Click on the area to highlight the WordArt and then click on the Format WordArt button and set Rotation to 180 on the Size Tab of the Format WordArt dialog box.

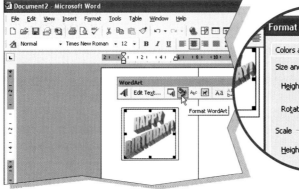

7 Now we'll add a message to the bottom-right quadrant, which will appear inside the card. Type the message into the text box in the bottom right of the page. Use Word's formatting commands to make the text appear stylish.

8 Don't forget Word's other features. Here, we've simply put in one of Word's pieces of clip art to add interest.

9 Once you've finished your card, just print the page and fold it in half vertically, and then horizontally.

PC TIPS

Word automatically adds outlines around each text box, which you might not want. To remove them, select all four text boxes and right-click on the shaded outline that appears. Select Format Text Box; then click on the Colors and Lines tab and choose No Line under Color in the Line section.

Setting up a mortgage account

Buying a home is possibly the most important investment you will make. Quicken can help you monitor your finances and budget for your future mortgage repayments.

In Stage 5 we showed you how to set up regular transactions, specifically your wages, for your main bank account (see Stage 5, pages 90–91). Here we will create a second account for a mortgage. Once you have set up the new account, you will find out how to enter the appropriate details about your home loan. Adding a new account is simple and allows you immediate access to the current balance of your bank account. Each Quicken account represents one element of your finances, so you can easily add new accounts for any type of loan or mortgage.

● **What you need to know**
At its simplest, an interest-only mortgage is a straightforward loan and can be very easy for Quicken to accommodate. But there are all sorts of mortgages providing different benefits that might be more difficult to represent. One such is an endowment mortgage, where an endowment fund is designed to pay off the loan at the end of the period.

Other mortgages where Quicken might have difficulty representing the benefits are those that are offered with an initial low-interest period. Quicken can still help here though, as you can see the effects of different interest rates by changing the interest rate values and then choosing the Calculate option, as shown in Step 5 opposite.

Before you start entering your mortgage details, make sure that you have all the paperwork to hand. For example, you will need to know when the loan started, the type of loan it is, its length and if there are any

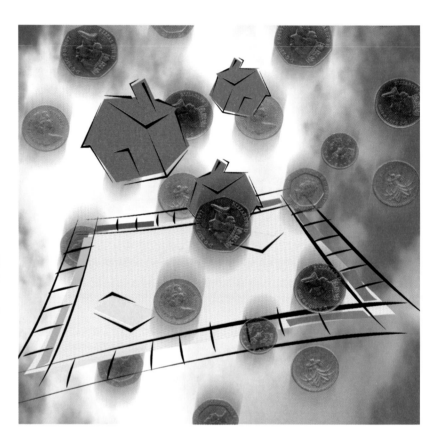

Whether you own a hotel in Mayfair, a house on the Old Kent Road, or even Fenchurch Street Railway Station, Quicken can help you calculate and manage your mortgage repayments.

final payments needed to clear it. If you are thinking of taking out a new mortgage, this exercise will help you to calculate your monthly bills and see if you can afford the repayments. To get an idea of current interest rates and special offers on mortgage rates, you can check out an online finance site, such as the award-winning www.motleyfool.co.uk, or an alternative such as www.moneyextra.com or www.moneysupermarket.com.

Once you have entered all the details of your regular outgoings into Quicken, it will help you to plan your future finances far more accurately. You can check that your cashflow covers the monthly bills and that you are making the most of your money.

TYPES OF MORTGAGE

There are many different types of mortgage. Quicken can handle most, including mortgages that require a lump-sum payment at the end of the loan. This so-called 'balloon' payment can be built into your Quicken mortgage account.

A new mortgage account

Here you'll see how to set up a new account and enter your mortgage details.

1 You set up a mortgage just like any other account. Start by opening the Property & Loan Centre by clicking on its QuickTab. Then click on the Create New Account button.

2 The next screen shows types of accounts that you can create. Select the House (with or without Mortgage) option and click on Next. Enter the information requested in the next few screens as they appear and call the new account 'House'.

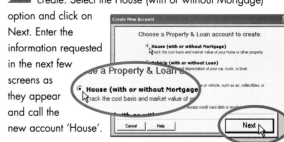

3 Since your mortgage has already started, you need to type in the starting point information. Progress through the screens, answering each question in turn. You can use the Back button if you make a mistake.

4 Type the length of the loan into the Original Length box. The Compounding Period (how often the amount of interest owed is recalculated) might be daily, monthly or annually. Then choose the Payment Period: most mortgages require monthly repayments.

5 Type in the interest rate for your mortgage. You can then enter the Payment Amount or Quicken can calculate loan payments for you if you select the Calculate option in the Payment area. When you click on Done, Quicken displays a dialog box telling you that it has calculated the values. Click on OK to return to the Edit Loan dialog box to see the calculated amount. Double-check these details before clicking on Done.

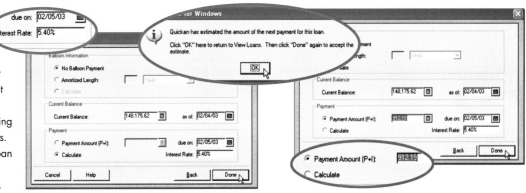

6 The repayment amount and next payment date are already entered for you. Just type a name for the mortgage in the Payee box – Include the lender's name, for example – and click on the OK button. Quicken may ask if you want to set up an asset account to go with the loan. Click on the No button.

7 The View Loans window displays the Loan Summary, Payment Schedule and Payment Graph. Should the interest rate for your mortgage change, you can alter the rate or any other information by choosing Loans from the Property & Loan menu. Then just click on the Rate Changes button to make the necessary adjustments to your Quicken records.

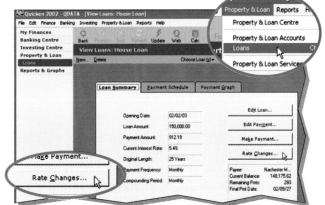

SHORT CUTS

Press [Ctrl]+[H] to display the View Loans window, to avoid having to hunt for it through Quicken's menus.

Graphs and reminders

To make sure you keep track of your finances and avoid money mayhem,
you can easily create graphs and automatic alerts with Quicken.

We've covered how to set up your main bank account with Quicken (see Stage 5, page 86) and how to create a second account for your mortgage (see pages 50–51). We have also demonstrated how to enter transactions into and out of your main bank account (see Stage 5, pages 88–89). Now we're going to show you how you can view and monitor these transactions.

We'll start by creating a graph that displays your bank balance over the course of the past few months. It's often easier to understand information when it's presented in graphic form, and your bank balance is no exception.

Quicken provides a range of tools that help you to create graphs based on different types of information from your accounts. Here we will create a graph to show how the balance of your account changes over time. This type of graph is useful when you want to check your cashflow to make sure that you have enough money coming into the account so you can pay all your bills on time.

● Choosing a graph type

As you work through the steps on the following pages, you'll see that there are several types of graph available, which are suitable for a variety of purposes. Some graphs, for example, can help you understand the figures from investment portfolios that display the fluctuating price of shares and how this affects your savings.

All the graphs work with the information stored in your accounts. You can view figures entered over the past year, month or quarter. If all you want is a quick overview of your account, you can use the Financial Calendar's Options commands (opposite).

● Expenditure analysis

One of the best aspects of a Quicken graph is that it analyses savings and expenditure. This is a great way of finding out the proportion of your income that you spend on various categories, such as entertainment or your

mortgage. To create this financial breakdown, you need to ensure that each entry in your account is stored under a suitable category – your electricity bill, for example, should be stored in the Utilities/Electricity category (see Stage 5, pages 88–89).

● Monitor your account

The graphs help you to see how your accounts fluctuate, but you can also get Quicken to keep a check on your account and draw your attention to problems. We show you how to monitor your account using Quicken's

Among Quicken's many useful features are ways of making graphs to see the bigger picture of your finances.

Intuit™ Quicken®

automated alert functions in the exercise on page 55. This warns you when you have too much money in your current account and should transfer it to your savings account.

The graphs also allow you to set up an automated alert that is triggered when your spending for entertaining, say, exceeds your budget for the month. The alerts work by monitoring the activity in each category of your account. You can set an alert trigger for any category from petrol to shopping.

● Categorize your transactions

Both of the exercises on the following pages – creating graphs and setting alerts – work by using category classifications linked to each transaction. Quicken includes categories that cover almost every main area of spending and income. Some of the major areas, such as utilities, are sub-divided into electricity, gas, water and so on. Each time you enter a new transaction in your account, make sure that you allocate it to the correct category (just use the pull-down list of categories when you're entering your latest transactions).

ADDING CATEGORIES

If you need to add categories to Quicken's list, you can edit or create new categories by selecting the Finance menu and choosing the Category & Transfer List command. This gives you complete control over the way you classify your income and expenditure, and helps you get the most from Quicken.

Creating a quick graph

Sometimes all you want is a quick, simple graph that shows you how your account balance is changing over the month. Rather than creating a complex graph, as we show on the next page, you can use Quicken's account graph function to get an instant view of your bank balance.

1 In the Register screen, open the account that you want to see displayed as a graph.

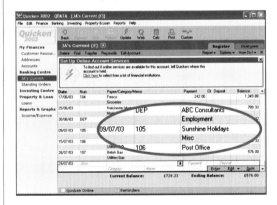

2 To select the Financial Calendar, click on the Finance menu and then select Calendar (see Shortcuts box).

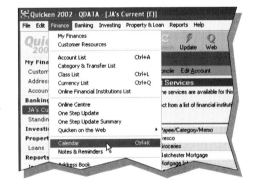

Press [Ctrl]+[K] to bring up the Financial Calendar without having to hunt through Quicken's menus.

3 You'll see the current month displayed. Click on the Options button near the top right corner and choose the Show Account Graph option.

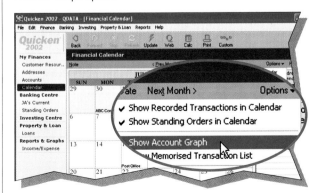

4 The window now divides into two and at the bottom you will see an instant graph displaying the pattern of your accounts balance.

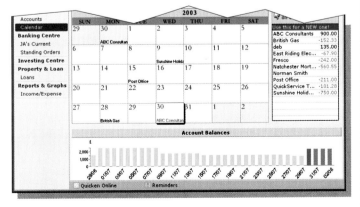

Creating a more detailed graph

It's often easier to understand information displayed pictorially instead of looking at sheets of figures. As its name promises, Quicken works fast at producing graphs that are readily understandable.

1 We've entered many transactions into and out of our current account. As you can see, the information is displayed in a basic ledger style. An easier way of viewing this information is to display the bank balance as a graph.

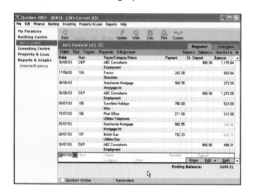

2 Click on the Reports menu and select EasyAnswer Reports and Graphs from the list of commands.

3 Quicken can display many types of graph based on your financial details. From the list of reports, select the option Where did I spend my money during the period...?, then click on the drop-down list next to For the period and choose the Last Qtr to see all transactions in the past three months.

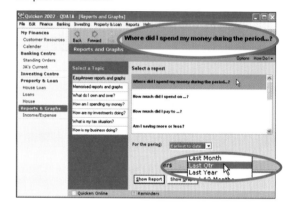

4 Click on the Show Graph button at the bottom right of the dialog box.

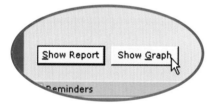

5 Quicken displays a bar chart of money flowing into and out of your account during the last quarter. To break down the quarter into months, select Month from the Interval drop-down menu and then click on the Update button.

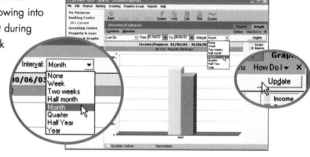

6 Our graph now shows the last quarter in monthly stages. There are several intervals to choose from — you could choose Year to see how this year's Income and Expenses compared to last year's, for example.

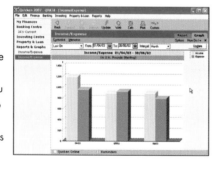

7 To get Quicken to show more detail, click on the Reports menu. Select EasyAnswer Reports and Graphs, then select How am I spending my money? from the list of topics. Select the Spending option and then click on the Create Graph button.

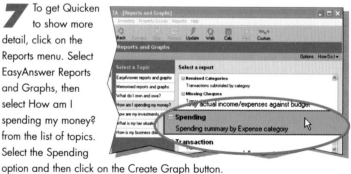

8 Quicken displays a pie chart along with a summary (inset right) of the way you spend your money. For example, you can see that the biggest utility expense over the quarter was the telephone, with the cost of the Mortgage forming the biggest expense of all.

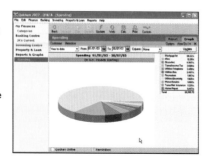

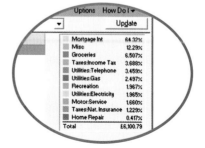

Create a calendar note

Remind yourself of important transactions by setting Notes & Reminders to appear each time you start Quicken.

1 To open the Financial Calendar choose Calendar from the Finance menu.

2 The Financial Calendar window appears. Click on the date to which you'd like to attach a note, then right-click and select Note.

3 Type your message into the dialog box and choose the colour of your notes. When you have finished, click on Save.

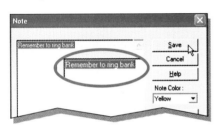

4 Quicken will then display a small, coloured box on the date. You can read or alter the note by clicking on it.

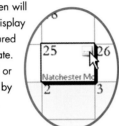

5 Click on the Edit menu and select Options then Reminders.

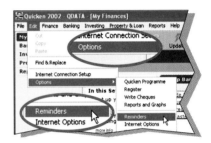

6 From the drop-down list, choose the duration you would like the calendar notes to display and then click on OK.

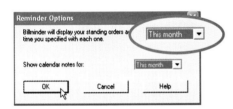

7 The next time you open Quicken any reminders or notes you have set up will be displayed in the Reminders window.

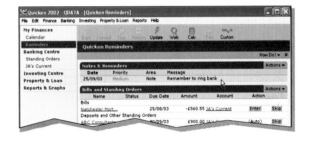

Setting a reminder

Set Billminder to display alerts and reminders automatically when you start Windows.

1 Choose Quicken from All Programs on the Start menu, then select Billminder. Note that you can't run Billminder while Quicken is open.

2 The Quicken Billminder dialog box appears. Click on Options.

3 To get Quicken Billminder to automatically display reminders whenever you start your PC, ensure Enable Billminder on windows startup is ticked in the Billminder Options box. Choose which alerts to display, then click on OK.

4 Finally, the next time you start your PC, the Quicken Billminder will automatically display the reminders and alerts you selected.

Quicken's Address Book

Once you get used to working with Quicken, you will find the Address Book a useful tool for organizing and storing contact information.

The Quicken Address Book is an ideal storage area for information you might need for your financial tasks. If you need to send out regular monthly cheques, for example, you can use the Address Book to print cheques and envelopes. The Address Book's group facility allows you to create lists, making this quick and easy. For example, you could create a group for 'Monthly payments' from which you can print the cheques, envelopes or labels you need on a regular, monthly basis.

● Add or update information
You can enter as much information as you l when you add a contact to the Address Boo As well as the usual details, the Address Record allows you to include personal information such as birthdays, anniversaries children's names, and so on.

The Address Book also contains the payee names and addresses you create when you u the Write Cheques, Standing Orders List or Memorised Transaction List. Changes you make to the contact information in the Address Book will show in your Memorised Transaction and Standing Orders Lists.

Deleting a contact only removes the information from the Address Book. It does not affect other information contained in Quicken such as your Memorised Transaction and Standing Orders Lists.

● Work with groups
When you add a contact to your Address Book, you can assign the contact to one or more groups. You can choose to use the groups the Address Book provides – such as Christmas List, Family, Friends or Work – or you can create your own. Quicken allows you to create up to 100 new groups of your own, and you can also edit group names or delete those provided.

Use the Quicken Address Book's group facility to take the hard work out of monthly printouts of labels and other stationery

The Modify menu gives you options for making the same change to several addresses at once. For example, click on Select All in the Modify menu to highlight everyone in your Address Book. Now you can use the menu's Format Address command to alter the way the addresses print out – such as making county and postcode appear on separate lines.

● Print from the Address Book
You might find it useful to print information from your Address Book, for example, a telephone list. When you print from the Address Book you can change the font and size, but you must first select the media you wish to use – labels, envelopes or just a list.

PC TIPS

Change the sort order
When you start to work with Quicken you will find that the Address Book is sorted by Payee. To change the sort order, click on the column heading that you want to sort by or select from the Sort list. For example, if you're planning to do a bulk mailing, choose Sort by Post Code.

Adding an address book entry

**Here we show you how to add an entry into your Address Book.
You can then print some or all of the contact information onto labels.**

Intuit™ Quicken®

1 To display your Address Book, select Finance from the menu bar and choose Address book.

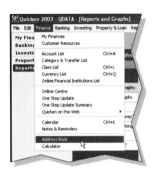

2 The Address Book window appears. To create an address book entry click on New.

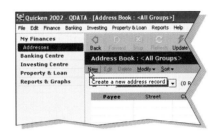

3 The Edit Address Book Record dialog box has five tabs within which you can store your information. When you add a record you must enter a payee name; any other information you include is up to you.

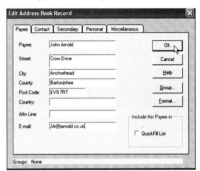

4 If you have entered a lot of records in your Address Book, you will find it useful to group your contacts information. With the relevant payee highlighted, click on Modify and then select Assign to Groups from the menu.

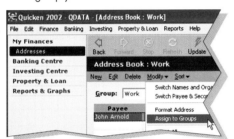

5 Quicken gives you the choice of four groups: Christmas List, Family, Friends and Work. Select Work and click on the OK button. You can enter the same record into several groups if you wish.

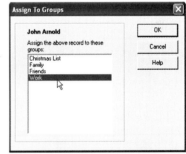

6 Now you will be able to see the entry when you select Work from the Group drop-down menu. You can also see that the group currently consists of just 1 Record.

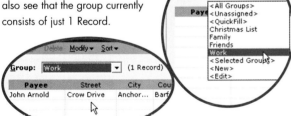

7 Should you want any additional groups, you can make your own by selecting <New> from the menu. In the New Group dialog box, type a name for your group and then click on OK.

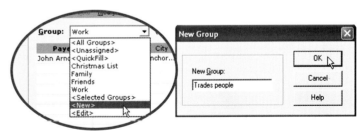

8 From within Quicken you can print some or all of the contact information stored in your Address Book. We want to print onto labels. Highlight the record in your Address Book, click on Print and then select Labels from the menu.

9 The Print Labels dialog box appears. Select your labels from the Print On list and enter the Row and Column number from where you want to start printing. We want to print an entire sheet of labels using this address, so select Return Address under Print Selection then click on Print. Finally, click on OK in the Print dialog box that appears.

Managing bank and credit card transactions

You can add extra accounts in Quicken to help you monitor your credit card spending and assist you in saving for special items. These new accounts work alongside existing ones.

So far, we have shown you how to set up your main current account (see Stage 5, page 86) and a mortgage account (see pages 50–51). You should now know how to enter transactions and create regular payments to and from your account. We'll show you how to link these accounts with other spending and savings habits – by setting up accounts for your building society savings and credit card.

● Added interest
Both savings and credit card accounts work in a similar way: interest is calculated on the balance at the end of each month and added to the total. In the case of a credit card, the balance is normally negative, whereas your savings account is positive.

Once you have followed the necessary steps and created your new accounts, you can use them in the same way that you use your main Quicken bank account. If you enter your credit card purchases as you use your card, you will know exactly how much you need to pay off the balance at the end of the month.

● Where is it all going?
When you record your credit card bills, you can use Quicken's ability to analyse your spending by organizing your bills into specific categories – entertainment, holiday, food or clothes, for example. To keep a close check on your spending, you can use Quicken's automated alert feature (see page 55) to warn you if a particular category, such as entertaining, exceeds its budget.

Credit card companies all use different interest rates – choosing the lowest interest

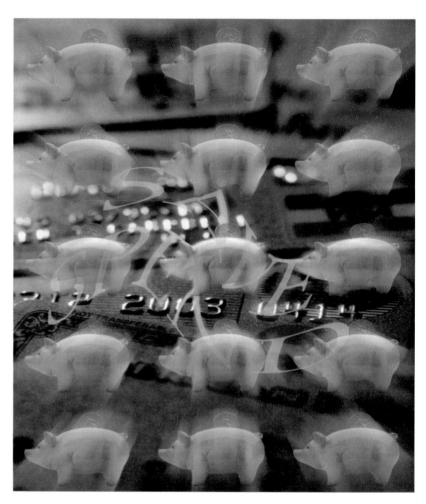

If you use Quicken to monitor your credit card account, you might be able to make some worthwhile savings.

rate is particularly important if you do not pay off your full balance at the end of each month. If you want to see the effects of changing from one type of credit card to another offering a lower interest rate, use the steps described on page 60 to see how your outstanding balance changes. You can use this feature to see how your credit card balance grows over a month or a year.

Saving rather than spending any spare money is never easy, but Quicken makes it simpler to organize your finances by letting you keep track of your savings accounts. You might have a savings account with a building society or with your bank and use this to generate interest on spare cash. Once you have set up your main savings account, you can use the same interest calculator that we use on the credit card account: this time it will show you how your money will grow over time at different interest rates.

One of the main reasons for setting up a savings account is to help you save towards a particular expense. For example, your goal might be to save for a special holiday, a new kitchen or car or, more mundanely, just to pay off a particular bill. Quicken makes it easier to work towards your goal by using its Savings Goal planner.

The Savings Goal planner asks you to enter your required final target and the date that it must be reached. It then calculates the amount of money you will need to save each month to reach your goal in the time specified. The main Savings Goal screen gives you

encouragement by displaying a progress chart. Although this feature sets up a new separate savings account, this is really just for ease of administration. You will probably keep all your savings in one account.

● **Keeping track of savings**
Your savings account, goal-savings account and credit card account all use the same method of recording transactions as your main current account (see Stage 5, pages 88–89). Once your new accounts are set up, you should find it much easier and more convenient to keep track of your finances. By moving money between accounts and using the interest-rate calculator, you will be able to your money work harder for you and be confident that you're earning the best rate.

Intuit™ Quicken®

Common steps when setting up new accounts

Many of the steps required to set up Quicken accounts are the same, whether it's a savings, credit card or mortgage account. Here, we'll set up a credit card account.

1 There are several ways to create a new account. One way is to click on the Create New Account button which is displayed in the Main View of the My Finances screen.

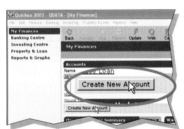

2 Quicken presents you with a selection of possible accounts. Click on the white circle next to Credit Card, then click on the Next button to continue.

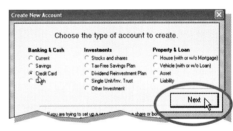

3 Enter a suitable name for the account – this will be used to identify it. Click on the Next button to continue.

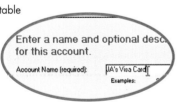

4 Quicken lets you handle multiple currencies in your accounts, although you will probably want to work in your own country's currency. Simply select the correct currency before clicking on the Next button to continue.

5 If you already have a statement for the account, Quicken lets you start the account with information from that statement. In this case, enter the Statement Date and the Balance Due, otherwise Quicken will use the current date.

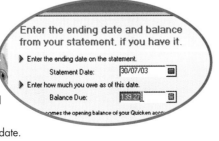

6 You are also given the facility to enter your credit limit for the account. If applicable, enter the amount in the box provided. Click on the Done button to finish.

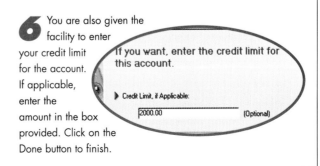

Monitoring your credit card account

Use Quicken's Reconciliation feature to keep track of how much you spend on your credit card and to check that your Statement of Account and your Quicken account tally.

1 Open the Credit Card account that you created on page 59. If you entered an amount in Balance Due and a Credit Limit (Steps 5 and 6), you will see that Quicken has automatically calculated the remaining credit.

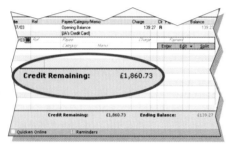

ACCOUNT ATTRIBUTES

Quicken's Account Attributes area is a convenient and handy place to keep information about your accounts. For example the account number, contact information and annual rate of interest can be stored here to make them easy to find when they're needed. To access it, click on the Overview tab near the top right hand corner.

2 Before you can begin to reconcile the account, you need to make sure that you've entered all your transactions, remembering to include any payments to the credit card company.

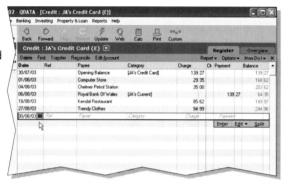

3 To reconcile the account click on the Reconcile button on the toolbar. Complete the Credit Card Statement Information using your credit card Statement of Account. Click on OK.

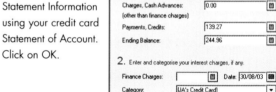

4 Quicken displays the Reconcile Credit Statement. On the left are your uncleared charges, on the right side your uncleared payments. You can adjust or add entries to match your statement. Tick each transaction from your statement in the left-hand Clr column and as you do, you will notice the Difference at the bottom (inset) changes. You and the statement agree if the Difference is zero. Finally click on Finished.

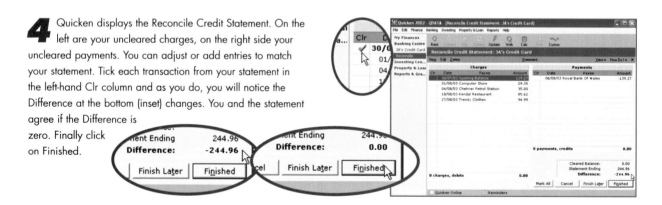

5 Quicken then displays the Make Credit Card Payment window, which allows you to make a payment. Select the Bank Account to pay from and the way you'll pay the bill. Then click on Yes.

6 If you have selected Printed Cheque, complete the transaction information and click Record Cheque. The cheque transaction is listed, added to your credit card account (below) and recorded against the account from which the payment comes.

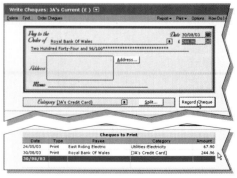

Transfer money between accounts

With Quicken you can transfer money from one account to another. Transfers record two transactions: one from the account where the money will be drawn and the other to the account receiving the money.

Intuit™ Quicken®

1 Begin by opening the account that you wish to transfer funds from. We've opted for JA's Current account. Click on the Transfer button.

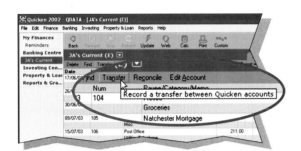

2 The Transfer dialog box appears. Select Create New Account from the drop–down list under To Account.

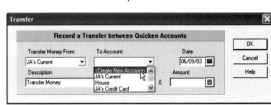

3 The Create New Account screen appears immediately – choose Savings and click on Next.

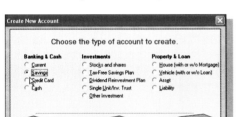

4 Work through the set-up screens following the steps as detailed on page 59, until you reach the window shown in Step 5.

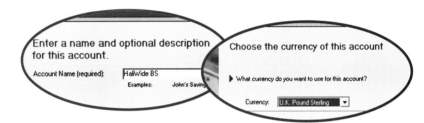

5 If your savings account will receive interest on a tax-free basis, click on the Tax button; otherwise click on the Done button. In the dialog box that appears, tick the Tax-Free Account box. Click on OK to return to the previous screen and click on the Done button to complete your new account.

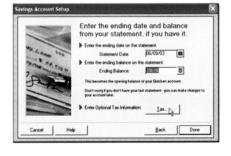

6 Enter the amount of money you wish to Transfer. Then click on the OK button.

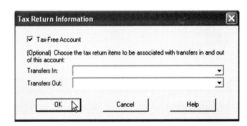

7 Quicken has registered the transaction in your current account. To view the parallel transaction in your savings account click on the Edit button on this transaction's row and then choose Go to Transfer.

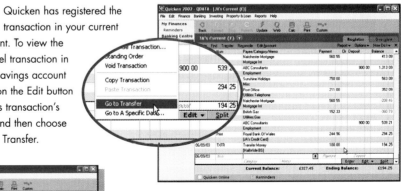

8 As you can see, the money has been successfully transferred to your savings account.

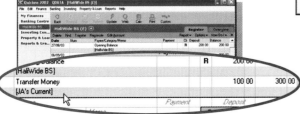

Balancing your budget

There are plenty of handy tools provided with Quicken. Among the most useful are the budget-planning features which can help ensure that you are always in control of your finances.

There are several tools provided by Quicken to help you manage your budgets. The first step, however, is to create a budget plan, and the best way of doing this is to focus on just one or two categories. We will use Groceries and Household and monitor these each month.

Before you start, you need to have an idea of the amounts you expect to spend on these categories. You will need to work out an estimate and set your month-by-month spending plans. Better still, you can let Quicken analyse the historical information that you've already entered and produce a basic budget for you. Your budget plan will provide the key foundation for your spending each month.

If you want to keep closer control over any particular individual categories, such as cash spending, eating out or entertainment, you could enter budget amounts for each, covering a two-week period.

For expenses that do not occur as often, such as electricity, water or other utility bills, you might find a quarterly or yearly budget easier to manage.

● Reporting features

Once the budget information has been entered, you can use Quicken's reporting features to monitor your real spending against your planned budget. It's best if you try to run a basic report on a regular basis to monitor the way in which your spending matches the original budget plan.

Another way to monitor your spending is to use Quicken's Progress Bar feature. This will display an instant view of how your finances are matching your planned budget.

● Planning your savings

You can just as easily use the budgeting feature to help you plan your savings. Apply the same techniques we look at here to plan for and monitor a category assigned to your savings. The budget function will enable you to exercise better control over all your finances – savings and spending alike.

It's easy for family finances to get on top of you, but with Quicken you have a means of keeping them under control.

Budget Goal Progress	Actions ▾
Utilities Budget 01/03 - 12/03 (£)	1,140.00
866.30	

You can use Quicken's Progress Bars to see quickly and clearly if you are managing to stay within your budgets. From the My Finances Centre, click on Customise and then Customise this view. Select Budget Goal Progress, click on Add and then on OK. Your budget progress will be shown in the main view of My Finances.

Creating a spending budget

Quicken will help you monitor how well you are staying on budget.

1 Start your budget by selecting Budgeting from the Banking menu.

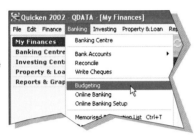

2 If this is your first budget you will need to select the Setup tab from the Budgeting window.

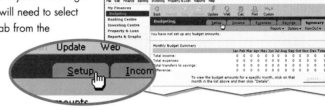

3 The simplest method is to get Quicken to create an automatic budget based on the actual income and expenses you have recorded in your current account. Make sure Automatic is selected and then click on the Create budget button.

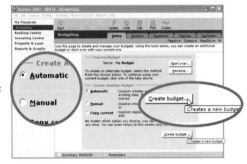

4 Now enter the dates Quicken will use as the basis for creating a budget from your previous transactions. Type the dates into the two boxes in section 1. Make sure Monthly is selected in section 2. Then click on the Categories button.

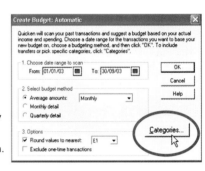

5 For the purposes of this exercise the only expenses we want to monitor are the Mortgage, Utilities and Groceries. So, click on the Clear all button and then put ticks next to Employment (income), Mortgage, Groceries and all Utilities except Water. Click on OK. You will then return to the Create Budget window. Click on OK again.

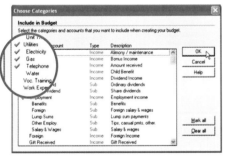

6 Your budget has now been created. You can see that the monthly average income exceeds our expenses by £345. To see a different viewpoint, click on the Options drop-down menu at the top right and select Combined View.

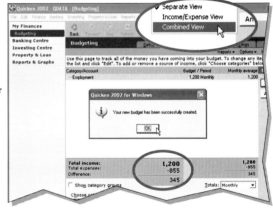

7 You can now see both the income and expenses breakdown. To see a summary of your budget click on the Summary tab.

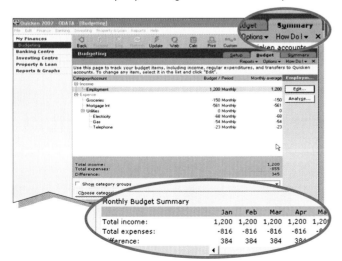

8 Click on the Reports button near the top right of the screen, and select Monthly Budget Report. When the report appears, you can see how you are performing in relation to your planned budget. The numbers in red in the Difference columns show where you've gone astray.

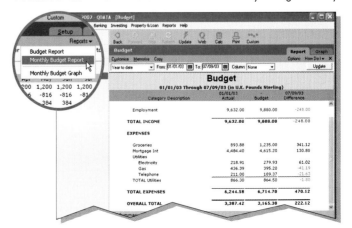

Introducing Microsoft Publisher

Producing documents that mix photographs and graphics with text is known as desktop publishing (DTP). Once the preserve of professionals, DTP is now accessible to all PC users.

With a desktop publishing program you can combine text, graphics and pictures in ways that make even dull documents look interesting and easy to read.

With desktop publishing (DTP), the emphasis is on the look of the document as well as its content. A desktop publishing program will give you a lot of control over the design and layout of your documents, providing very precise positioning of all the elements that make up the publication.

The good news is that DTP today is easy, especially with the help of Microsoft Publisher – one of the best desktop publishing programs for the home PC user.

● Success in phases

The desktop publishing process has four essential phases. In phase one you plan your publication. You decide on the physical size and shape, the purpose, content and the overall design, and how it will be printed and/or distributed.

In phase two you assemble most of the elements that you'll need. This might mean text, illustrations, photographs, logos, clip art and so on. You don't need to be too rigorous about getting them all before you start as extra items can be added later. Publisher can import files produced by most common word processors and graphics packages. You can also generate material as you go. For example, you can type in text directly and then scan in various images. Publisher also has some handy drawing tools for graphics creation.

In the third phase you set up Publisher and start working. Publisher comes with a large collection of ready-made template designs for just about any kind of publication. It's best to use one of these templates unless you really can't find one to suit you. There are plenty to choose from and you don't have to stick with every aspect of the template's design.

In the fourth phase you save your document and publish it, which might mean printing it, saving it in a format a professional printer can use or publishing it as a Web page.

● Trying out templates

Using a template is easy. You select the overall design and then Publisher's Quick Publication Options let you customize the template's elements. You can also add specifics, such as illustrations and text. When you become more experienced, you'll be able to customize the standard templates and to use the amended version as a new template.

● Choosing your layout

You don't have to start with templates, of course. With a blank sheet of paper you can easily decide how wide you want the margins to be, how many columns of text you need, where any headlines, blocks of text and graphics should go, and so forth. The same principle applies to a blank Publisher workspace. However, it is easier in the beginning to use or adapt one of the standard Publisher designs.

● Installing Publisher

As with most Windows software, installing Publisher is quite simple. Insert the CD-ROM in the drive and the Publisher Setup routine should start immediately. If it doesn't, open your My Computer folder and double-click on the icon for your CD drive; that should start the setup process.

Installation is then a matter of following the on-screen instructions. You will need the CD key (the 25-digit reference on the back of the CD case). You will also be asked to choose a folder in which Publisher should be installed. The best option is to follow the suggestion offered.

You are also asked to choose between a Typical and a Custom installation. It's best to choose the Typical installation, however, as that copies most of the files you are likely to need. This option calls for around 180MB of

hard disk space. If you choose the Custom option you'll need less space as you can decide which Publisher components to install, but, unless you're sure of what you need, it is better to install everything. With the latest version of Publisher you have to activate the program to register your copy with Microsoft by telephone or Internet. You must do this within the first 50 times of starting the program, or it will stop working. Microsoft has also taken this anti-piracy measure with Windows XP (see Stage 1, page 29).

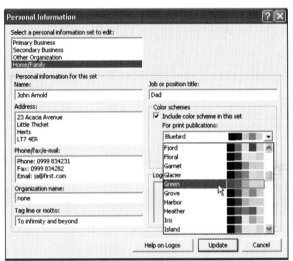

When you type your address and contact data into Publisher's Personal Information dialog box, you can also opt for a preferred colour scheme to use in your publications at the same time.

● Saving

It's a good idea to save your work every five minutes or so, because Publisher won't do that automatically for you (it can, however, pop up a note every so often to remind you to save your publication). To set this up, click on the File menu and select Save As. In the Save As dialog box, type a name for your publication in the File name box and then use the Save in box to choose the folder where you want to store it.

If you don't yet have a folder to store your Publisher documents, it's worth creating one now so that these don't get mixed up with other documents. To do this, click on the Create New Folder button on the small toolbar at the top of the Save As dialog box. When the file name and folder are correct, click on the Save button.

If you accidentally forget to save your document when you close Publisher, it will ask you if you want to save it. Click on the Yes button to save it or click on the No button to discard it, or to revert to the previously saved version.

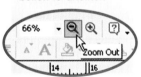
GETTING STARTED WITH PUBLISHER

When you have installed Publisher from the CD-ROM, you'll find that a Microsoft Publisher entry has been added to the Programs list on the Start menu. Click on this and Publisher will load.

At first, the workspace in Publisher is divided into two panels, with a Task Pane on the left and a panel of Publisher's Quick Publications, or templates, on the right. The Quick Publications panel lets you see small previews of the ready-made designs that are included with Publisher.

If you want to use any of these Quick Publications, you

can click on a preview. Publisher instantly creates a new document based on the template you have chosen, ready for you to alter to create your own publication.

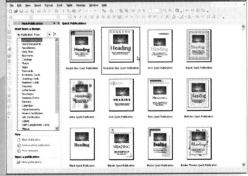

Using Publisher

Once you have Microsoft Publisher up and running, it's easy to find your way round its uncluttered display. Almost all of the tools will seem familiar to computer users who are acquainted with other Microsoft programs such as Word or Excel.

THE BEST way to learn about a new program is to use it. Here we show you the main components of the Publisher window and on the next page we begin with a simple exercise. If the Task Pane is taking up too much of the program's display area on screen, you can easily hide it by clicking on the cross in the top righthand corner.

THE OBJECTS TOOLBAR AND THE PASTEBOARD

The Objects toolbar is a quick way to get the elements you need, such as clip art, boxes for text, photographs and shapes you have drawn yourself, to the workspace. You don't have to commit them to a final position on the page: use the pasteboard area to collect items that you might want to use and then drag them onto the page when you're ready. The pasteboard's contents stay the same when you move from one page to another, so anything you haven't used on page one might find a home on a page further into your document.

Standard toolbar

This will be familiar to any user of Microsoft programs – it contains buttons for the common commands such as Save and Print.

Menu bar

All the Publisher functions are accessible from the menus under these commands but, for easier access, many are duplicated by buttons on the other toolbars.

Zoom controls

Magnify the workspace (the publication and pasteboard) by clicking on the plus button, reduce it with the minus button, or enter a specific percentage.

Margin guides

Even a blank document like this one has these non-printing guides. When a frame edge is close to the guide, the frames will 'snap' to fit the guides exactly.

Formatting toolbar

This is greyed out if no object is selected (as here), but normally it provides a quick way to change the look of text, graphics and so forth.

Objects toolbar

These buttons let you add different kinds of objects to a publication – such as pictures, shapes and boxes for text.

Page controls

Each page of your publication appears as an icon. The current page is highlighted in blue. Clicking on a page switches to that page.

Pasteboard

The area all around the actual page can be used for temporary storage of text or graphics elements while you're deciding where or how to place them.

Publication

The inner white space corresponds to the printable area, so all finalized text and artwork should be placed in this area.

Creating an advertisement to display in a shop window

Publisher can handle both big and small DTP tasks. Here we demonstrate the program's capabilities as we create a postcard advert that will be displayed in a newsagent's shop.

1 Click on the Start button then All Programs and then click on Microsoft Publisher. Select By Blank Publications in the drop-down menu in the Task Pane and select the Postcard template. Click on the preview to create your blank postcard.

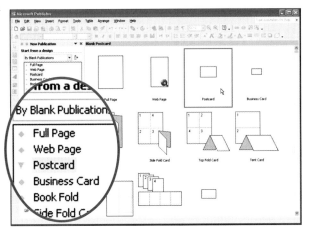

2 The blank postcard appears in the workspace to the right of the Task Pane. Now click on the Text Box tool.

3 Place the cursor at the top left point of the inner (blue) margins. Hold down the right mouse button and drag the cursor down and towards the right to create a box for the headline. Release the mouse button when the box is about a quarter of the way down the page and has touched the right-hand margin (it will 'snap' to fit the margins exactly when you draw close enough to them).

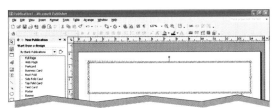

4 When you release the mouse button a cursor will appear in the box. Type the text, 'Holiday home to let'. Press [Ctrl]+[A] to select all the text in this box.

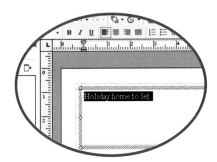

SHORTCUTS

Checking your publications for spelling mistakes is a vital part of the DTP process. It's well worth developing a simple keyboard shortcut routine before printing your documents: before pressing [Ctrl]+[P] to start printing, press [F7] to start the spell checker.

5 Use the Formatting toolbar to change the font settings to Arial, bold and centred. If you can't see the Formatting toolbar, click on View, then Toolbars, and put a tick against Formatting. Now go to the Format menu, click on AutoFit Text and then select Best Fit.

6 To draw another text box filling up the rest of the space on the card, click on the Text Box tool and then drag a box shape from the bottom of the headline to the lower right corner of the frame. Type in the rest of your text and press [Ctrl]+[A] to highlight it. Increase the type size to 16pt so it stands out and then centre the text.

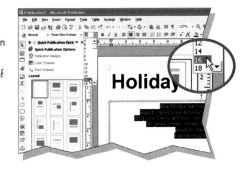

7 You might need to resize the boxes to ensure that all the text is visible. Click in any box. The white circles that appear on the edges of a frame are called grab handles. Position the cursor over one and it changes to a two-way arrow. Click and hold down the mouse as you drag that part of the box one way or another. When you release the mouse the text will reflow to fit the new shape.

8 Use Publisher's built-in spell checker. Click in one of the boxes, select all the text, and click on the Tools menu, then Spelling and then Spelling again to activate the spell checker. When you've finished, save and print the postcard.

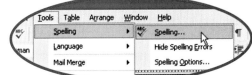

The New Publication Task Pane

Publisher's handy New Publication Task Pane presents lots of useful designs and templates that you can use in your new document.

When you start Publisher, the New Publication Task Pane appears by default, although you can bypass this (see the PC Tips box, below right).

The drop-down list box at the top of the New Publication Task Pane window offers three different ways of working:
● By Publication Type (the default option) – ready-to-use templates, organized by type so that, for instance, all newsletter designs are grouped together.
● By Design Sets – templates organized by style so that different types of publications can be given the same basic look.
● By Blank Publications – layouts with no design features which are intended to suit different sizes of paper and folding methods.

● By Publication Type

When you select By Publication Type, the Task Pane lists types of document, such as Labels or Newsletters, on the left. Clicking on one of these will display previews of the templates available in the larger area on the right. The currently selected preview has a blue border.

Each template has a range of options that appear in the Task Pane once you have clicked on the required Publication Type. These options cover basic layout and design choices, to give your publication a unique look.

● By Design Sets

With By Design Sets selected, Publisher lists collections of documents with one basic style so a business can create a range of corporate stationery. The first option, Master Sets, offers collections of documents with styles which can easily be adapted to your needs. The other options are geared to specific applications.

The last group of templates, Special Paper, is intended for use with a range of pre-printed papers from Paper Direct (see page 79). You can also use the templates with ordinary blank paper, but the effect is not as striking.

Publisher's New Publication Task Pane offers a wide range of designs, document types and layouts which you can put to good use.

● By Blank Publications

These templates are useful if you are happy to create your own designs from scratch, as they save time setting up documents to suit a particular size of paper or special fold (such as greetings cards made from A4). There are no design elements or objects on the layouts, but all the margin guides are already in place to help you to position your objects within the printable area on the layout.

● Existing files

If you want to open a Publisher document that has already been created, you can click on the More publications option at the bottom of the New Publication Task Pane. Use the Open Publication dialog box to select your document.

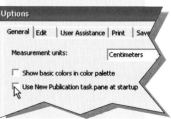

Create your own templates

Adapt one of the New Publication templates to suit your needs.

EACH TIME you use any of Publisher's ready-made templates from the Task Pane, you'll have to set up the basic styles for colour schemes, logo placements, number of columns and so on. Once you have decided on an overall look for your documents, however, you can easily create and save templates of your own. To do this, follow the steps below to edit one of the New Publication templates. You can then save the results as a template, which means that you can't overwrite it by mistake, before adding the final text and graphics desired for individual documents.

Microsoft® Publisher

1 Select By Design Sets from the list box at the top of the New Publication Task Pane. In Master Sets, select a template from the set on which you want to base your design. In this case, we will be adapting the Newsletter template in the design set called Blocks.

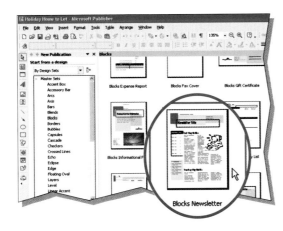

Blocks Newsletter

2 The Task Pane now shows options for customizing this document. For example, select a colour scheme for your personalized template. If you want to create a consistent look, use the same one for the newsletter and any other documents for which you want to create templates.

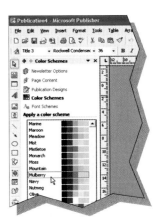

3 Use the other options in the Task Pane to make other changes, such as the number of columns you want for your publication. Here, we have selected a single column format.

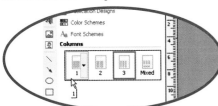

4 As well as the options set by the Task Pane, you can apply different text formats. Select the headline, for instance, and choose a font from the drop-down font menu. This will be used each time you open the template.

5 Carry on choosing text formats until you are happy with the style of your template. Then select Save As from the File menu.

6 Give your template a name (such as newsletter). Now select Publisher Template from the Save as type box at the bottom of the dialog box. Click on the Save button to save the file.

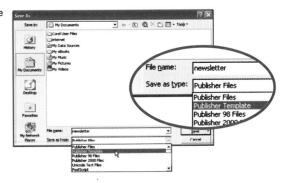

7 When you want to use the template you've just created, simply open the New Publication Task Pane and click on the From template option at the bottom of the dialog box.

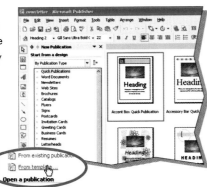

8 Publisher will look for all the templates you have saved. Your new Newsletter template is there ready for use, together with any others you have already set up.

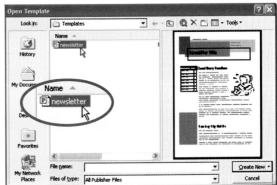

Designing with the Task Pane

When you are creating a new document based on one of Publisher's ready-made templates, you'll find plenty of time-saving options on the Task Pane.

The Publisher templates listed in the New Publication Task Pane are complete sample publications. Each one contains basic formatting for a particular type of document, including the size and shape of the page, the way the text and graphics are arranged, the colours for the background and text, the styles for the text and paragraphs, and so on.

● Instant professional designs

Different types of publications have different options in the Task Pane. Because of this, it's important that you check to see what's listed here, even if you haven't found the options for other templates useful. Once you explore these options, you'll have a complete and ready-to-use document.

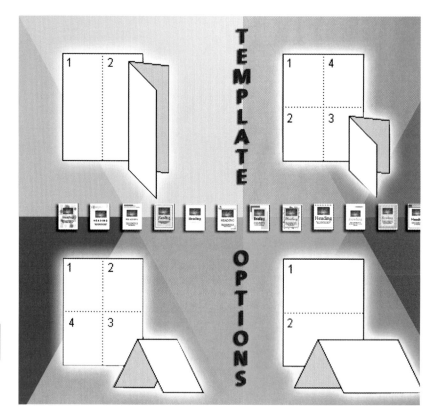

The templates in Publisher are ready-made foundations upon which you can build your finished document.

These templates are easy to personalize by adding your own text and, perhaps, some graphics. You can also make further design changes but, unless you're confident about your designing skills, you probably shouldn't make too many changes until you have more experience of working with layouts.

● A consistent style

Sometimes you won't want to produce just a single document. If you run an organization – a small company, a club or a school, for example – you'll need several types of document, such as headed paper, a newsletter, invitations and business cards. These should all have the same overall style to emphasize that they're from the same source.

Publisher recognizes this need, so the By Design Sets listing on the New Publication

Task Pane is arranged by style, with different sets of publications sharing the same overall design. Common elements include colour schemes, fonts and repeated logos.

You don't have to close the New Publication Task Pane if you want to open one of your publications. To quickly open the last publication you worked on, try looking for it at the bottom of the New Publication Task Pane. If you have edited the file recently, it will probably be listed here. If it isn't listed,

click the More publications option. This displays the Open Publication dialog box, allowing you to browse the files and folders on your hard disk and open any Publisher document you've previously saved. Alternatively, you could click on the File menu and select from the list of recently used files at the bottom of the menu.

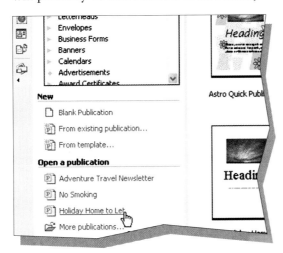

Documents you recently used are listed at the bottom of the Task Pane so that you can find them again easily.

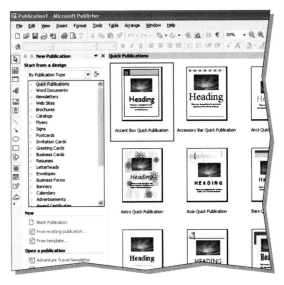

The New Publication Task Pane displays previews of the templates that come with Publisher, making it easy to find a design that you can modify to create your own documents.

Using Help

Publisher offers extensive help facilities at several levels to suit users' differing needs.

THERE ARE two basic ways to get help in Publisher. First, the Office Assistant is a friendly helper which pops up if you click on the question mark button on the Standard toolbar. Type your question, click on Search and the Assistant will return a list of topics that match your question. Click on the most relevant one to get a full answer.

You can also start the Assistant by pressing the [F1] key or by going to

the Help menu and clicking on Show the Office Assistant.

The second type of help is provided by Microsoft Publisher Help, which you can select from the Help menu. When the Help window comes up, browse through the topics listed under the Contents tab and more detailed options will appear. To search for something specific, click on the Index tab and type in a relevant word. Then just click on Search and Publisher will list all the topics containing the word you typed.

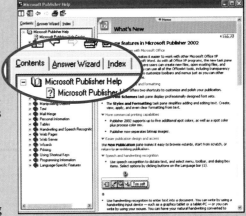

Three tabs on the Publisher Help window let you browse or search for advice and information on hundreds of topics.

Using Mr Clippit, the Office Assistant, is as easy as typing in your question in plain English.

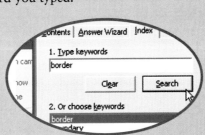

Creating a postcard with the Task Pane

We show you how to use Publisher's Event postcard template in the Task Pane to create a smart publicity postcard for a school fête.

1 In the New Publication Task Pane, select By Publication Type from the list box. A list of templates appears below the list box. Click once on Postcards. A list of different postcards will be displayed.

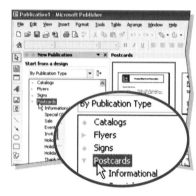

2 Click on Event and a selection of postcard designs will appear in the right-hand window. The first Event postcard will have a selection box around it. Use the scroll bar to move down the designs. Click on the Blackboard Event Postcard.

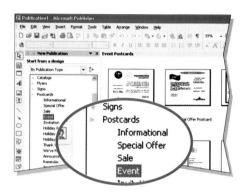

3 The postcard template will appear in the main window, and the Task Pane changes from listing new publications to providing options for your document.

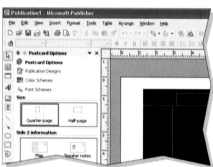

4 You can explore these options in any order. For example, click on Color Schemes and the Task Pane changes to list many ready-made schemes. Click on any of the schemes to see how it affects your design.

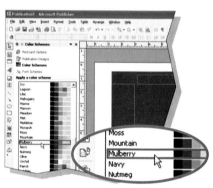

5 The Postcard Options let you choose one of two sizes for your postcard – either a quarter or half of an A4 page. The quarter-page is nearer the standard size for a postcard, so select that.

6 Each side of the postcard is an individual page. To see the other side of the postcard, simply click on the page 2 icon at the bottom of the screen. This side of the postcard also contains text. You can use the Font Schemes options to try combinations of text styles to save having to modify each one yourself.

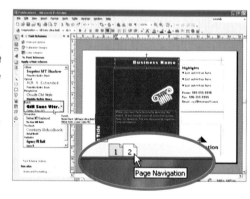

7 With your basic postcard complete, you are ready to start working on the text and pictures on the page. First save your document by using the Save command on the File menu, so that you are ready to begin the exercise on the opposite page.

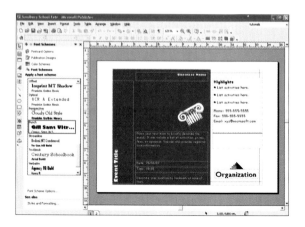

PC TIPS

Hiding the Task Pane

The Task Pane takes up a small space in the Publisher window, and most of the time it's worth displaying it. However, to maximize the work area, you can hide it. Click on the small X button at the top right of the Task Pane.
　　To make it appear again, select Task Pane in the View menu.

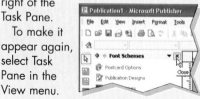

Completing the Postcard

The basic postcard is now ready for you to fill in details of the school event and to add your choice of graphics.

1 If you examine the document created previously, you will see that it contains lots of dummy text but that Publisher has entered some information automatically – the organization's name, in this example. This is easily changed.

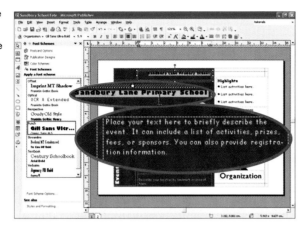

2 The existing text is there just to indicate what goes where. You can change each block by editing or replacing it. To do this, simply select the words you want to change and start typing. Anything you type now will replace the selected text.

3 Repeat this for each block of text on the page, including the vertical type, which you can treat as normal horizontal text that just happens to be displayed on its side.

4 Now click on the page icon at the bottom of the screen to go to page 2, which is the address side of the card. Change the school's address on the upper left. Delete all other text (apart from the stamp guide box) by right-clicking on it and selecting Delete Object from the pop-up menu.

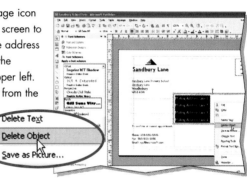

5 Go back to the message side (page 1) by using the page icons again. We're going to replace the classical image with something more appropriate. Place the mouse-pointer over it and double-click.

6 The Insert Clip Art Task Pane appears. Type 'tent' into the Search for clips box, and press the [Enter] key. Click on a picture and select Insert from the menu that pops up. You might be asked to insert the Publisher CD-ROM.

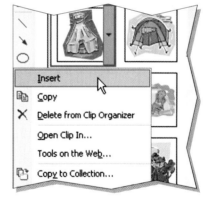

7 The new tent image will replace the classical portico but only a white silhouette appears initially. Right-click on the tent image, select Format Picture and when the Format Picture dialog box appears, click on the Recolor button. Click on the Restore Original Colors button in the dialog box, then click on OK.

8 Save your work now and take a look at the finished article. To see the postcard without the non-printing outlines and guides, go to the View menu and click on Boundaries and Guides. Then make any further changes you want. Don't forget to save your work at regular intervals.

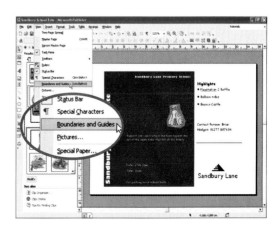

Printing your documents

The whole point of using a desktop publishing program is to produce professional printed copies. So, as you might expect, Publisher gives you plenty of print options.

The print options you choose depend on exactly what sort of finished document you need. Most of the options are used to control your desktop printer, as we show on pages 76–77, but you can also save a printable file on disk so that you can have a high-quality version produced by a specialist commercial print shop.

● Setting up the page
Before sending a document to a printer, you need to set it up the way you want. Page Setup in the File menu provides basic options, including page orientation – vertical (portrait) or horizontal (landscape) – and folding choices. You can also print pages that are larger or smaller than standard A4 paper. A postcard, for example, can be positioned in the centre of the paper ready for trimming, while a banner can be printed on multiple sheets and stuck together.

● Setting up the printer
Other print options are available via the Properties button in the Print dialog box (see Stage 1, page 105). The default settings are the same as those entered in the Windows Printer Properties dialog box when connecting a printer and include paper size, orientation and source (how sheets are fed into the printer). However, the Properties dialog box lets you alter these settings to suit your publication.

Properties settings override those in Page Setup, so you can get a business card to print out on a portrait page, even if its own Page Setup is landscape. However, you are more likely to want to change the Properties settings to match the way that you have arranged the pages of the document. Any changes you

make apply only to the current publication – the Windows Printer Properties aren't altered and the Properties settings for one publication do not affect those used in other documents.

When you print a document using the Print command on the File menu you get a range of options (see The Print dialog box, opposite).

● Printing large quantities
If you need anything more than a few copies of a document, you have a number of options:
● You could run them out on your printer, but this might prove to be slow and expensive. The choice of paper is also limited; business cards, for example, are best printed on card but this might not pass through your printer.
● For medium quantities (up to 100 copies of a single-page document), using a good-quality photocopier could be an economical solution.
● For larger quantities and anything printed on special paper or card, your best bet may be a print shop or commercial printer. Such companies can work with almost anything you bring in, but you will get the best results and a cheaper service if you set up the Publisher document properly.

Documents produced using Microsoft Publisher have a great deal in common with publications designed for commercial printing. In fact, you can arrange to have your Publisher documents professionally printed by supplying suitable files directly to a printing company.

● **Preparing files for a printing service**

Many printing services will work from a paper original produced by your own printer, but you will get better results if you give them the document on a zip disk. They can then print it using their own, superior equipment.

Even if the printing company does not have a copy of Publisher, you can use the File menu's Pack and Go commands to create a file that it can use. A wizard leads you through the process, including a handy checklist and points to discuss with the print shop.

To help simplify the process of getting your publications printed by a professional printing company, the Pack and Go command collects all the necessary files, pictures and fonts into a single file that you can provide by email or on disk. Before taking this step, however, it's well worth finding a local company that can handle Publisher files. Some printing companies focus on commercial desktop publishing programs and might not be able to work with Publisher.

If you can't find a local printing company that can output the files created by Pack and Go, you can use PostScript files instead. PostScript is the industry standard for professional printing but it is a little more complicated. Click on Publisher's Help command (see page 71) to search for information about creating PostScript files.

PRINTING IN BOOK FORM

There are several options for preparing small booklets using your own printer. You can print single-sided sheets and staple or clip them together, or even produce double-sided pages by reversing the paper to print alternate pages. However, this is very fiddly, so it is easier to take single pages to a local copy shop which has equipment that will produce back-to-back prints; they can then bind them for you too.

If your booklet has small pages (no larger than half the size of your paper), you can print two of them side by side on a sheet and fold the pages together. With A4 paper, you can fit two A5 pages on each side, making a total of four pages in all (right). To see the full range of folded print-out options available, select Page Setup from the File menu. If you then select Folded card in the Publication type panel of the Page Setup dialog box you can choose from several ready-made folded paper booklet forms.

The Print dialog box

Here are the options accessed via Print in the File menu. Additional printer settings are controlled by Page Setup.

Printer
Choose a desktop printer from the drop-down list. The Properties button lets you change the specified printer's settings. Select the Print to file option to save the document in printable form, rather than print it immediately.

Print range
Choose to print all the pages in the document, the current page (the one you can see) only or a specified range of pages.

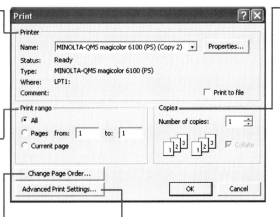

Copies
Specify how many copies to print and whether a multi-page print run should be collated by page number or printed in order.

Change Page Order
Click on this button if you want to change the way Publisher prints multiple copies of your document. For example, you can print multiple copies on a single page and get Publisher to work out the best spacing for them. This button does not appear with some documents.

Advanced Print Settings
Click on this button if you want full control over the way that your documents print. You can turn crop marks (which indicate where the paper must be trimmed) on and off and choose whether to print graphics or not. Commercial printers can also set different colour separation options here.

Setting basic printing options

Here we show how to adjust the print settings to cope with a document that is a horizontal (landscape) format and smaller than an A4 page.

1 Open the document that you want to print. We've selected a simple No Smoking sign.

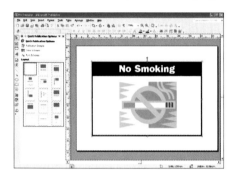

2 With the document on the screen, click on the File menu, then on Page Setup. This document is a special size and at 25x18cm is slightly smaller than A4. Make sure the Landscape option is selected to ensure that it will be the right way round on the page. Click on OK.

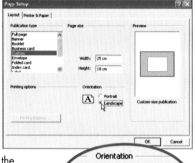

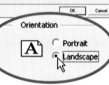

3 Go back to the File menu and select Print from the commands available.

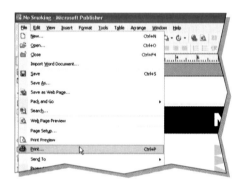

4 Select your printer from the list in the Print dialog box, if it isn't already the default selection. We have chosen a laser printer with a black-and-white A4 output.

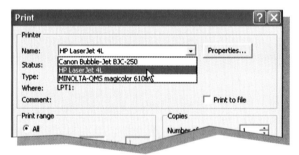

5 Specify the pages you want to print. In this case it's a one-page document, so you could click on either All or Current page.

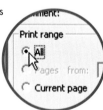

6 If you want more than one copy, enter the appropriate number in the Copies section to the right of the dialog box.

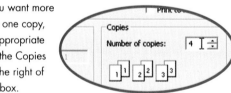

7 Click on the Advanced Print Settings button.

8 At 25x18cm, the document is smaller than the A4 paper used by the printer, so tick the Crop marks box (below) to print thin lines showing where the document should be trimmed. Click on OK and the printer will produce four copies of the sign, ready for trimming.

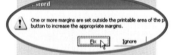
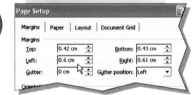

Better printing on a colour inkjet

Here we look at the best way to use a desktop inkjet printer to print out a newsletter that has been created in full colour, including photographs.

1 First, open your document – here we are using a newsletter. With the publication on the screen, click on the Tools menu, then on Options.

2 Click on the Print tab and select Print line-by-line. This gives better results with an inkjet printer, although it is slightly slower. Click on OK.

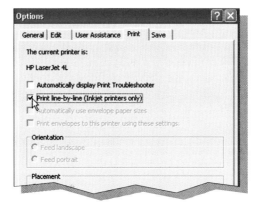

Microsoft® Publisher

3 Click on the File menu, then on Print. Select the printer you want to use, if it isn't already selected. We are using an Epson colour inkjet.

4 Click on Properties. This brings up the Properties dialog box for your selected printer. Make sure the Paper/Quality tab is selected. This has settings for the type of paper, ink and print quality. Select Best from the Quality Settings to choose the highest quality print mode and then make sure Color ink is selected.

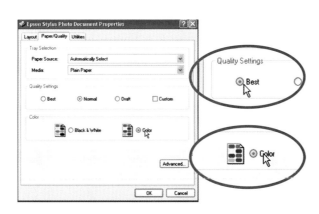

5 Click on OK to return to the Print dialog box. You also need the pictures to print out at the best quality, so click on the Advanced Print Settings button and in the Print Settings dialog box, select the Print full-resolution linked graphics option. Click on OK to go back to the Print dialog box.

6 Select the print range and the number of copies to be printed (see Steps 5 and 6 on the previous page), then click on OK to start printing.

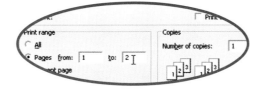

Create your own letterhead

Just because you're using templates, your letterheads and other stationery needn't look identical to those of every other user of Publisher. Here we show you how to alter the templates to your own design.

Letterheads give your letters an impressive, professional look, and if you're running an organization – whether it's a small business or a social club – a good letterhead is essential.

Publisher comes with a range of standard letterheads, but you can also personalize them to create your own distinctive designs. You then simply take your design to a local printer to get as many sheets as you want printed up. You can use the printed letterhead paper either for hand-written letters, or to slot into your printer for printing from the computer – taking care that the text you're printing doesn't overprint the design.

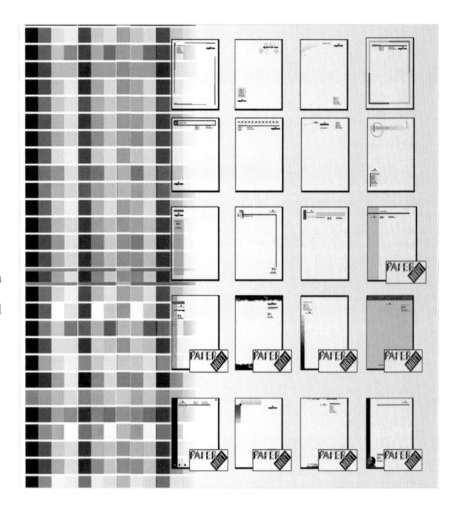

● Heading the field

The quickest and easiest way to get started with a new Publisher design is to use one of the ready-to-go templates from the New Publication Task Pane. You'll see several of these listed under By Publication Type.

You might choose to design other documents besides a letterhead, for example, business cards, a fax cover sheet, price lists, brochures, or newsletters. It makes sense, therefore, for all your documents to have the same design, look and 'feel'. Publisher's design sets were created for this purpose.

With Publisher, there are templates to suit most types of stationery. You can base yours on ready-made designs, or create your own personalized version.

Microsoft Publisher's templates make it easy to create successful business stationery very quickly, from newsletters and letterheads to business cards and catalogues.

Microsoft® Publisher

PC TIPS

Objects
Nearly everything you put in a Publisher document is called an object. Each of the elements of a template design is an object, and anything you add to it is also an object. Objects in Publisher include:
- logos
- photographs
- other graphics – stripes, patterns and coloured bars
- blocks of text.

Each of them gives you a coherent look for a collection of different documents. Typically, this means using the same colour scheme, logos and other graphics for each of the basic elements. The Publisher design sets give you a starting point that you can adapt to create your own unique style.

● Special paper
Two types of letterheads are shown in the By Publication Type list: Plain Paper and Special Paper. The Plain Paper designs assume that you'll use your own blank paper. However, some specialist suppliers produce attractive ready-coloured and patterned papers, and Publisher has a collection of letterhead templates designed for the range of papers created by Paper Direct (call 0800 616 244 for a catalogue or visit the website www.paperdirect.co.uk).

If you select the Special Paper option, the screen displays a range of designs suitable for coloured and patterned papers from Paper Direct.

The elements of a Publisher design set

Here is part of the collection from the design set called Blends. Although the elements are different, they all have a similar look. The same style of logo, for example, is used for each type of document, and it appears in the same place on the page in relation to the other design elements.

Newsletter

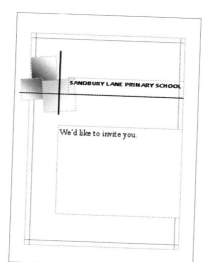

Letterhead

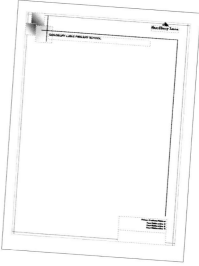

Product leaflet

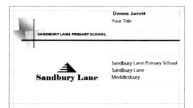

Business card

Compliments slip

Creating headed notepaper

Designing a basic letterhead with Publisher's templates couldn't be a more straightforward process.

1 Start Publisher and in the New Publication Task Pane, click on By Publication Type from the drop-down box. Look down the list of publications until you find Letterheads. Click on it and select Plain Paper.

2 Click once on the Blocks Letterhead template and the letterhead design will load up.

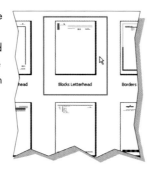

3 You now have the letterhead design on the screen. You can use the Task Pane options to customize the basic layout with the colour scheme of your choice, add your own logo and implement your own font scheme. To start, click on Color Schemes.

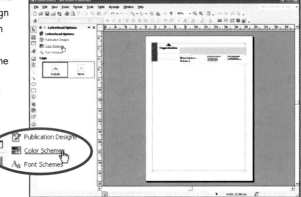

4 This design starts with a default colour scheme called Sunrise. Move your cursor down the list of other schemes and see how the colours on the page change. When you find a colour scheme you like, click on that. We have selected the colour mix called Mist.

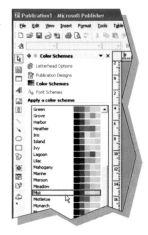

5 By clicking on Letterhead Options, you can choose whether or not to include a logo.

6 Next, click on Font Schemes to apply a font scheme of your choice. We've opted for Modern.

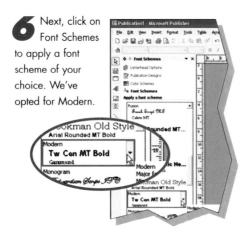

7 You might not be able to see all the detail on the design. To enlarge the picture so that you can see what's going on, click on the Zoom In button on the right-hand side of the toolbar.

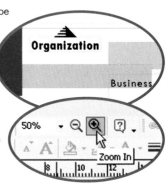

8 The Task Pane will stay on the screen, so you can make changes to your selections at any time. To enter your address, click in the address frame, position the text entry point and type over the text with your address details. The spellchecker might query words that are not in its dictionary by underlining them in red, but the underline will not print out.

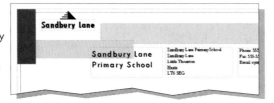

9 Select Save As from Publisher's File menu to save your work. Choose a suitable folder in the Save in box, type a file name into the File name box and then click on the Save button.

Personalizing your letterhead design

You can make your own headed paper using Publisher's templates, and with just a few simple changes to the template it's easy to create your own unique look.

1 Publisher's templates help you get a quick start on your letterhead, but without some customization, your design is likely to look like many others, and may not fully suit your needs. Start by opening your letterhead.

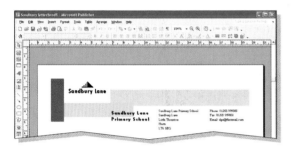

2 In our example, we want the full name of our school to be more prominent. To make sure it's the first thing people will see, click on the box that contains the name and drag it to position it above the longest horizontal block in the graphic, so that it is above the other letterhead details.

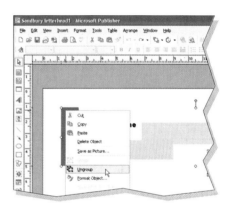

3 To make the name fit on a single line, drag the small circle that appears on the middle of the left edge of the box further to the left. When you release the mouse button, the text automatically reflows inside the box.

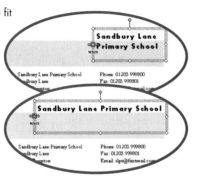

4 You can also alter the way that the colour scheme is applied to the graphic. In this example, the colours are fine, but the long bar is a dull grey. To try out different colours, first right-click on the blocks graphic and select Ungroup from the pop-up menu.

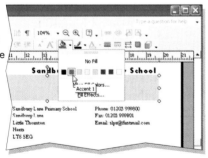

5 Now you can select the individual rectangles used in the blocks graphic. Select one of these boxes and then click on the arrow just to the right of the Fill Color button on the Formatting toolbar. The pop-down panel shows the colours in the current scheme. Choose a new colour and repeat the process for other objects.

6 You can also alter the size of the logo. However, before doing this, bring the logo to the front (see Order and text wrap box, below). To do this, click on the logo and then click on the Bring to Front button on the Standard toolbar.

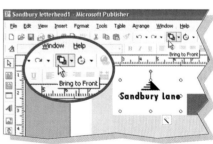

7 Now drag one of the white circles that appear on the logo's corners to resize the box. Experiment to get the best size and position for the text and graphic in your logo, and adjust the other text elements to get a good visual balance. Save your letterhead when you have finished.

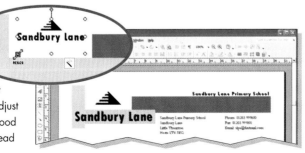

ORDER AND TEXT WRAP

In the Publisher template, the logo sits behind the blocks of the graphic. It is necessary to bring the logo to the front of your design – as shown in Step 6 – so that it is on top of the blocks. If you don't do this, the text in the logo will try to wrap around the blocks instead of sitting in front of them when you increase the logo's size in Step 7.

Using text frames

Publisher uses frames to hold all the different elements of a publication – including text, pictures, tables and logos. Text frames are especially versatile because they can be linked, allowing what you have written to flow from one frame to another through the document.

Publisher holds both text and images in frames. These are rectangular containers that can be sized and positioned on the page. Before any element can be placed in a Publisher document, a frame has to be created within which to place it.

The software provides several different kinds of frame: one to hold text, another for tables and a choice of three for graphics. There are different options and considerations for each type of frame. For example, text might need to be laid in columns within a text frame, whereas picture frames are dictated by the size and shape of the images.

● Controlling text position

You could think of text frames as imaginary boxes that Publisher can size and place wherever you want on the page. You can even put a frame on the pasteboard outside the document as a temporary storage facility.

Publisher sets up each of its pages with rectangular guidelines. If you create a text frame and move it towards one of these guides, the software will automatically 'snap' the edge of the frame to the guideline once you get within a millimetre or two.

The simplest kind of Publisher document uses each frame as a box that fills most of a page, with the text laid out inside it in a similar way to a word processor. As each page has its own text frame, they need to be linked so that as soon as there is too much text for one frame, it will run into the next.

Publisher can automatically add new pages with linked text frames. This works in exactly the same way as a word processor, adding extra pages to a document as you enter more text. Alternatively, you can add more frames whenever they are needed, but you need to link all the frames manually so that the text can flow on. Publisher provides linkage tools to enable you to join frames in any sequence you want, and you can also break links that you have set up.

● Flowing text

Text is normally inserted in a frame as if it were a miniature page in its own right: it starts at the top left and ends at the bottom right. You can add as much text as you want. When there is more text than a frame can hold, the overflow symbol (A…) appears and you can then delete the extra text or create a new frame to hold it.

If you insert additional text part way through a document, Publisher will push the following text down to make room. An overflow symbol will appear if a new frame is needed. Similarly, if you delete some text, the words that follow the deletion will flow back as far as necessary, through all the linked frames.

Once text frames have been set up within a document, text can be placed in them. If suitable links are created, a long piece of text can be made to flow from one frame to the next. Publisher will even print a message to tell you when it runs over to a new page.

Microsoft®Publisher

FRAME POSITION

Frames are normally moved into position with the mouse but you can also move them in precise, small amounts by using Publisher's nudge facility. To do this, select the frame, hold down the [Alt] key and press the arrow keys in the keypad to move the frame in the direction you want, a fraction at a time.

You can also use the Zoom facility to help put a frame exactly where you want it – for example, to make sure you are placing the edge of a paragraph precisely in line with a picture. Such precision in placing text is simply not possible with a word processor.

● Displaying frames

The edges of each frame are shown on screen by dotted lines that do not print out. However, if you want a border that prints out, you can add one at any stage. We cover the process of adding decorative lines and borders later.

A document can contain many text frames, so to make things easier for you, the one that you are working on is highlighted with a shaded outline containing small white circles called grab handles. These appear at each corner and midway along each side. You can drag the grab handles with the mouse pointer to resize or reshape a frame.

Publisher uses mouse-pointer symbols to indicate what type of operation is occurring. For example, if you are resizing a frame by clicking on its grab handles, the cursor changes to a double-headed arrow, or when moving a text frame, the cursor becomes a small van icon. The program also shows links between frames with a chain and indicates text insertion with an image of a pouring jug.

● Positioning text in a frame

Your text doesn't need to fill a whole frame up to the edges – you can create a border inside the frame. You can also decide what you want to happen when another frame is placed inside, or partially overlapping, a text frame.

Desktop publishing allows you to make text in one frame flow around the edges of another frame. You can alter this 'runaround' feature to suit your needs, for example, to create a wider or narrower margin around a picture or a bold headline inside a panel of text.

However, text doesn't have to run around an inserted frame. In the case of Publisher's watermark feature, one frame can hold a background image which will show through any frames placed on top. You should think of multiple text frames as layered, one above another, onto a document's surface, like Post-it notes stuck on top of each other. You can alter the order in which they are layered by bringing individual frames forwards or backwards.

If you move a frame, the text inside moves with it. You can rotate a frame (and its text) to any angle. You can also cut, copy and paste a frame and its contents. This is often the easiest way to produce a short piece of text in a particular format – simply by pasting over the original.

On pages 84 and 85, we show you how to lay out and link text frames, and how to put in continuation notices.

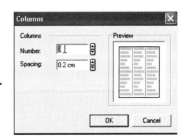

Publisher's five frame tools appear on the Objects toolbar. The A in a box denotes the Text box Tool.

Handling multiple columns

To improve the appearance and legibility of long lines of text, your document may need more than one column per page.

THERE ARE two ways to include columns when you are setting up a Publisher document layout, both of which use text frames. The first option is to create a single frame filling the whole area in which you want to put the text. You can then specify that the text inside the frame is arranged in columns. This is the best method to use when you want the text to appear in side-by-side columns of equal width, as the frame will simply be divided equally into the number of strips you choose.

When you have drawn the text frame, right-click on it and select Format Text Box, then click on the Text Box tab. Click on the Columns button and enter the number of columns you want – the preview image will confirm the effect of the change.

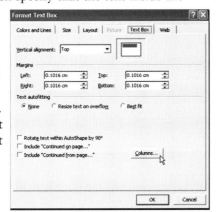

The Format Text Box dialog box lets you alter the way Publisher fits text into a box.

The Columns dialog box lets you set the number of columns you want and the space between them.

The second method is to draw more than one text frame, setting up one for each column. You can then link the frames using the frame linkage tools, so that text flows from one to another. This method of creating multiple columns makes it easy to produce columns of different widths. It is also easier to use if you want to specify variable spacing between the columns or if they need to start at different heights on the page.

Laying out text frames

Here's how to position text frames by using column guides. We also show you how to deal with text overflow from the first frame by linking it to a second.

1 Start a new blank publication. To set up two column guides, click on the Arrange menu, then Layout Guides and type 2 in the Columns box. As shown in the Preview window, dotted outlines will appear on the page to indicate two columns. There will be a small gap between these two columns when you return to your document. Click on OK.

2 Click on the Text Box Tool and draw a frame across the top of the page for your text heading. Readjust the size using the corner grab handles. The frame will snap to the nearest guide as soon as you get close to it.

3 Type some heading text and format it. Now draw a text frame inside the left-hand column guides and below the heading frame, so that it snaps to the guides. Repeat the process to draw a second frame filling the right-hand column.

4 Click in the left-hand frame to select it. From the Insert menu select Text File. Locate a file that contains lots of text and click on OK to import it. When it pours into the frame and overflows, the overflow symbol (inset) will appear at the bottom. Click the No button when Publisher asks if you want it to use autoflow to create extra text frames.

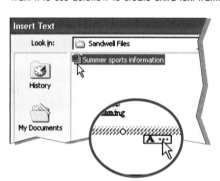

5 To make text flow from one frame to another you need to use the Connect Frames toolbar. You can normally find it at the far right of the Standard toolbar (inset). If you can't see it on your PC, select Toolbars in the View menu and then click on Connect Frames.

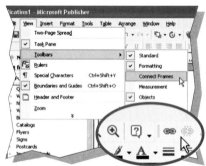

6 Make sure that the left-hand frame is still selected – its corner grab handles should be visible. Now click on the Create Text Box Link button on the new toolbar and the cursor will change to a jug. Move it into the second frame and click again to 'pour' the text. If the text is too long to fit into the second column, the overflow symbol will appear again.

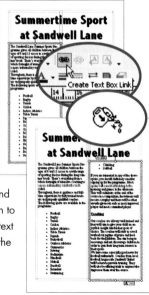

7 To add another page for the overflow text, select the Insert menu and then select Page. Type '1' in the Number of new pages box, click on the After current page option and then click on OK.

8 Draw a text frame on the new page. Return to the first page, click in the right-hand column to select it, then click on the Create Text Box Link button again. Go back to the second page and pour the overflow text into the new text frame. Carry on creating new pages and text frames in this way until all the text can be seen.

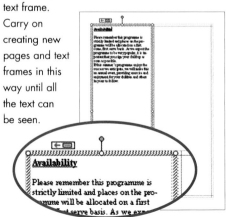

Adding continuation messages

Continuing the exercise that we began on the previous page, we show you how to insert automatic 'Continued' messages where text flows from one frame to another.

1 To add a 'Continued' message, go back to page one of your document and right-click in the right-hand column. Select the Format Text Box option.

2 When the Format Text Box dialog box appears, click on the Text Box tab. Tick the Include "Continued on page..." option. Now click on the OK button.

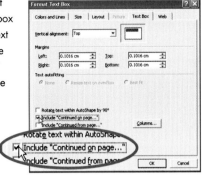

3 A 'Continued' message will appear at the end of the frame. Publisher automatically inserts the relevant page number and will adjust it automatically if the pagination of your document changes.

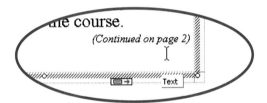

4 You can change the wording of the message. Drag the cursor over the text to highlight what you want to change but don't include the page number or it will cease to be updated automatically. Now type in your preferred wording. You can also add text after the page number or delete the brackets.

5 You can alter the size, typeface, text colour and other properties of the 'Continued' message. Highlight the text (this time you can include the page number) and use the text formatting buttons on the Publisher toolbar to select options such as bold, italic, alignment options and typeface.

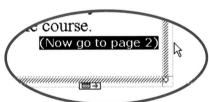

6 Go back to page two and right-click on the text frame there. Select Format Text Box and then the Text Box tab from the dialog box that appears. This time, tick the Include "Continued from page" option.

7 Click on OK and '(Continued from page 1)' will appear at the head of the frame. It will have the default text formatting but, again, you can select the text to alter this and/or the wording, as in Steps 4 and 5.

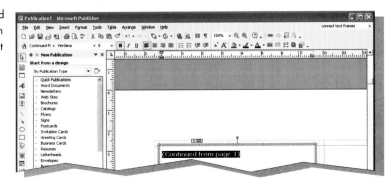

'Continued' type style

Altering 'Continued' messages one by one to a different type style is not too much of a chore if you have only a small number of them in a document. However, in order to avoid this often repetitive task, Publisher lets you set a new default style for all 'Continued' messages.

First select a 'Continued' message and format it to the new style that you want. Select this text, then select Styles and Formatting from the Format menu. The Styles and Formatting Task Pane appears. Click on the small arrow to the right of either the Continued-From Text or the Continued-On Text styles in the Task Pane and then select the Update to match selection option.

Importing graphics and text

You can easily add text and graphics created in other programs to your Publisher pages. This saves you time and allows you to create a greater variety of documents.

Microsoft Publisher allows you to produce both text and simple graphics directly in your publications. You can use the drawing tools, for example, to produce boxes, circles, ovals and straight lines. However, you might also want to use material produced by other programs. You will need to import this material into your Publisher document.

● Importing text

Whenever you need to import text, you can use Publisher's text acquisition feature to save yourself time and laborious re-typing. Microsoft Publisher can import all of the common word-processing formats, which means that you should be able to insert text from more or less any text file.

The value of importing text is not simply that you transfer the words straight into your document, but that you should also be able to import any formatting the author has applied. That includes bold or italicized text and in most cases you will also retain paragraph indents, bullet lists, text alignment and perhaps even tabbing. All these built-in features will make your task much simpler.

Publisher will also do its best to retain named styles created for the original text. This allows you to adjust the style to change the formatting for all text to which that style was originally applied.

● Old frame, new text

To import text into an existing text frame you first need to move the text insertion point to the place where you want to insert the new

material. Then use the Text File command on the Insert menu, and locate the file which contains the text that you want to insert.

You can also create a brand-new frame into which you can import text. Click on the Text Box tool button in the Objects toolbar and the crosshairs will appear. Next, hold down the left mouse button and draw your frame, release the button and the cursor will be positioned at the start of the text area, ready for text to be inserted. See pages 82–85 for more information on using text frames.

Publisher enables you to build complex documents by bringing in text and graphics from a range of different sources.

PC TIPS

File and image formats

As there are dozens of different formats for text and graphics, Publisher is not able to recognize every one of them, though it does handle all the common formats.

Virtually all word processors can save text in a variety of formats, so you should be able to ask the originator to save the document in one of the generic formats – .RTF is a reasonable all-round option. Most programs that produce graphics give you a choice of image formats, so go for something Publisher can read – try either a .BMP or .JPG format.

Publisher can automatically flow extra text into new frames if the existing frames are too small for the text being imported. This is called Autoflow and you will be asked if you want it to take place. If you click Yes, Publisher will look for the next empty text frame and will ask if you want text to flow into it.

Where there are no more text frames Publisher will ask if it should create one; clicking Yes causes Publisher to create text frames on as many new pages as are needed to fit all the rest of the text.

● Inserting graphics

Microsoft Publisher can also insert graphic images into special, non-text frames in your document. For example, clip art can be placed in a clip frame using the Clip Organizer Frame on the Objects toolbar. The Clip Organizer is part of Publisher, so accessing this range of pictures is very simple.

If you wish to use a picture from another Publisher document, the Edit menu's cut and paste commands are ideal for copying the picture into your document. This is also the method you would use for copying a picture from a document in another application, such as Word or CorelDraw. For example, to copy a bitmap picture that has been used in a Word document, you would open Word and copy the picture to the Windows Clipboard (see Stage 1, pages 16–17). In Publisher, you can then simply paste the picture from the Clipboard into your document.

Graphics can be stored as images on disk, for example, CorelDRAW includes a collection of images stored as CDR files. Publisher has an Insert picture facility (see page 89) which prompts you to select an image from a folder on your disk; the image is then placed in the picture frame in your document.

● Acquiring images

If you have a scanner attached to your PC, you can illustrate your designs by scanning in artwork or other material. You have two options, the most direct option being to scan the image straight into a picture frame that you've already added to a Publisher page. This uses a Twain interface (see Publisher and scanning box, below). However, once the image has been scanned into the picture frame, there's little you can do to change anything other than its size.

For this reason, most DTP users take the other approach, first scanning the image into a graphics program such as Corel PHOTO-PAINT. The image can then be retouched as necessary and saved on to the PC's hard disk. Once this has been done, the picture is imported into a Publisher picture frame using the Insert picture command.

● Finishing touches

In Publisher, text will automatically re-flow where a picture or clip-art frame overlaps a text frame. You can adjust the gap between the picture and the text to make sure that the text is easy to read.

Finally, a line can be placed around the picture to give it a border and to separate it from the text.

PUBLISHER AND SCANNING

Publisher can control a scanner directly, allowing you to scan an image without having to exit the program. A special interface, called Twain, has been developed to allow this. To tell Publisher that the source of an image is a scanner, select Picture from the Insert menu and then choose the From Scanner or Camera command. This command asks Windows to bring up the Twain scanning software installed on your PC. The scanner's control window will open on the screen, allowing you to scan as usual.

Your scanner will give a preview of the scanned picture on screen. Confirm that this is the picture you want and Publisher will place it in the document.

How to import text

Here's how to add some emailed text to a Publisher document that deals with the Carter family's history.

1 For the purposes of this exercise, you can use any Publisher document – we've chosen a family history document. Open the document using Publisher's Task Pane.

2 Click on the document and it will be opened in Publisher's workspace. You are going to insert a new page to import some text that has been cut and pasted from an email using Notepad (see pages 24–25).

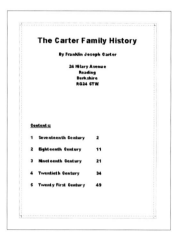

3 Select Page from the Insert menu and type '1' in the Number of new pages box. Select After current page, ensure Insert blank pages is selected in the Options list and then click on OK.

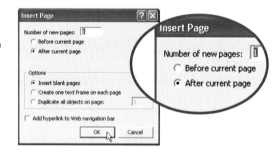

4 A new blank page will appear. It needs a text frame to hold the new text from the email. Select the Text Box tool from the Objects toolbar.

5 To make a text frame, position the cursor (now crosshairs) in the page's top left corner. Click and hold down the left mouse button, dragging the pointer to the page's bottom right corner. Release the mouse button and the text box will fill the page.

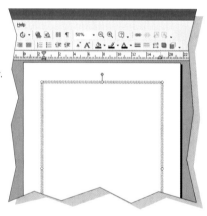

6 To insert the new text, click on Text File on the Insert menu. Then use the Insert Text dialog box to find the email text from the folder you used to store it. When you've found it, select it and click on OK.

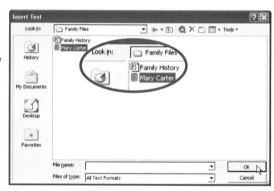

7 The text now flows into the frame you have previously drawn, starting from the top left-hand corner. The email formatting is preserved.

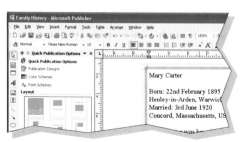

8 Edit and format the text to fit in with the look of the rest of the document. We have enlarged and centred the heading and initial details, and started the main text with a drop cap. To do this, click anywhere in the first paragraph and select the Drop Cap command from the Format menu.

Inserting a picture

A digital photo that has been copied to the hard disk now needs to be inserted into the family history document.

1 Open the family history document. You are going to place a picture on the right-hand side of the first paragraph.

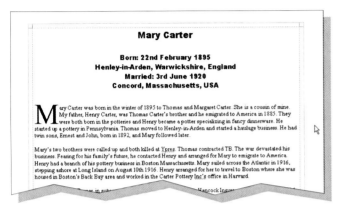

2 Click on the Picture Frame tool in the Objects toolbar. Use the mouse cursor (now crosshairs) to draw a picture frame to receive the image. The Insert Picture dialog box automatically pops up.

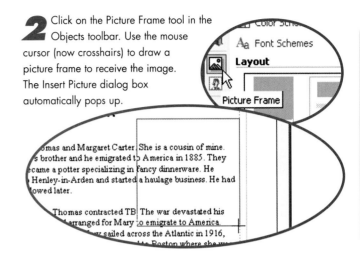

3 Locate the picture image file on the hard disk and select it. Publisher will display a thumbnail-size preview so you can check it is the right one. If it is, click on the Insert button.

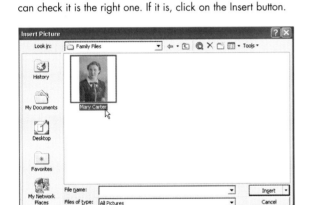

4 The image will now appear in the picture frame in your document. Although the text flows around the picture frame, it does touch the picture in some places.

5 To keep the text away from the edge of the picture, right-click on it and select Format Picture. In the Format Picture dialog box, click on the Layout tab and set 0.5cm margins for all sides.

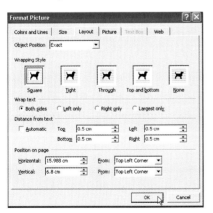

6 The document would also look better with a border around the picture. Click on the Colors and Lines tab and select a suitable Color and Style for your picture frame outline. Click on the OK button.

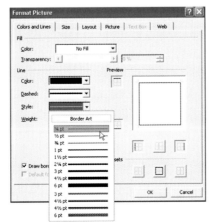

7 The finished document now has a boxed image set apart from the surrounding text which flows neatly around it.

Creating a Master Page

For lengthy documents, it's best to use Publisher's Master Page to add repeating elements to your pages. These objects appear automatically on each page of your document.

Save time, brighten up your pages and maintain consistency through your document by using text and graphics in the background.

One-page Publisher documents, such as posters and leaflets, are easy to create – all you do is add the objects to the page. However, longer documents benefit from a bit more forethought. With planning you can ensure that you don't waste time adding the same elements to each page in the document.

In addition to the foreground of the document, which contains your text and graphics, you can apply standard elements to every page as part of its background using the Master Page feature. Imagine a sheet of transparent plastic overlaid on a piece of paper: if you add objects to the paper (Master Page), they will be visible through the plastic (foreground).

● Repeating objects

Any objects you add to the Master Page will appear on each page of the publication. Consequently, Master Pages are ideal for page numbers, repeating logos, running headers and footers similar to those in Word (see Stage 2, pages 44–45), ruled lines and so on.

The foreground remains the place where you do most of your work – where the document's main text and images are laid out – but a Master Page is the best way to give each page of your publication a consistent look.

● Building a Master Page

On the Master Page you can use the same elements that you can put into the foreground:

text, clip-art images or photographs, rules or boxes. You can use any size, shape or colour that you want. For example, you can add a full-page coloured rectangle on the Master Page to add a colour tint to each page of your document. You can also add a watermark – a faint image or message behind the objects on your page – such as a company logo or a text stamp saying CONFIDENTIAL. Using a Master Page ensures that all the variable factors, such as size, shape and orientation, are the same, page after page.

● Hiding the Master Page

Publisher will automatically use your Master Page on all pages in the document unless you tell it not to. If you want to switch off the Master Page for a particular page, go to that page and click on the View menu. Select the Ignore Master Page command and the Master Page will be removed from that page. You can always reinstate it if you change your mind.

Designing a Master Page

A Master Page can range from a full-page tint to simple lines of text, such as headers and page numbers, as below.

1 Start Publisher and, on the New Publication Task Pane, select By Blank Publications. Next, click on Full Page to create a new, empty page.

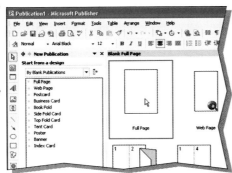

2 Click on the View command and select Master Page from the menu. The document display doesn't seem to change, but the 'R' page icon at the bottom left of the screen tells you that you are now working on the Master Page.

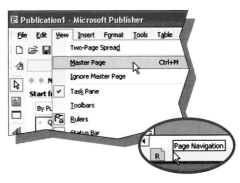

3 Enlarge the page by changing to a zoom setting of 50%. Add a text box just above the blue guide lines at the top of the page by clicking on the Text Box tool and dragging the mouse from left to right.

4 Inside the frame the cursor will be blinking. Type the text for a repeating header, using Publisher's text formatting tools, such as the Center button on the toolbar, to adjust the look of the text.

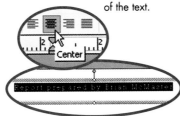

5 Draw another text box at the bottom of the page and type the word Page followed by a space. Then select Page Numbers from the Insert menu and click on the OK button in the Page Numbers dialog box. A # symbol appears next to your text. Publisher will repeat this on each page, at the same time as changing the # symbol to the appropriate page number.

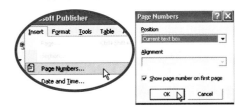

6 Highlight the page-number text and click on the right-align button. Choose a different typeface for the text to make it stand out.

7 Add another text box to the left of the page number and type: ALL INFORMATION ON THIS PAGE IS CONFIDENTIAL. This text will be repeated in the same position on every page.

8 Click on the View menu and select Master Page to go back to your document. The Master Page elements are visible, but you can't edit them unless you switch back to Master Page mode. Note that the page numbers appear automatically in your document.

HOW MASTER PAGES WORK

The longer the document, the more likely it is that a Master Page can help to save time and effort. Here we show you how spending some time setting up a single Master Page means that a long, arduous design process doesn't need to be repeated every time a new page is added to the document.

A Master Page can contain your repeating design elements.

This means that the foreground pages can be kept simple, which makes them easy to edit.

The completed publication combines both. Consistency between pages in the style and layout of objects is guaranteed.

Adding personal data

Many of your documents will use the same information time and again - your name and address, for example. Fortunately, Publisher has a way to add standard elements quickly and easily.

Publisher helps you to create documents efficiently by letting you store short pieces of standard text (and even a logo) in what it calls personal information sets. The stored data can include anything from your address to a slogan you regularly use on business documents. Once you have entered the text, you can use it as often as you want. This saves the trouble of retyping and eliminates the danger of spelling errors and omissions (as long as you've got it right the first time).

When you install Publisher, the personal information set contains default data. This consists of your name and company, if you typed in these details when you set up the program. However, you can change or add to this text at any time. To do this, you need to open a publication, call up the personal information, edit it to give the appropriate details, then save it as the default. Your changes will be stored in the selected personal information set, and will be available the next time you open any Publisher document.

● Different sets of information

Each Publisher document offers four personal information sets, called Primary Business, Secondary Business, Other Organization and Home/Family. They all provide slots for address text, plus another slot to use if you want to add a logo. A new document offers the Primary Business set by default but you can easily swap to one of the others.

Primary Business is intended for the regular letterhead of a company. The Home/Family set is used for personal text, such as your home address. The other two sets can be used for the more occasional, specialist needs of a business or an organization such as a club.

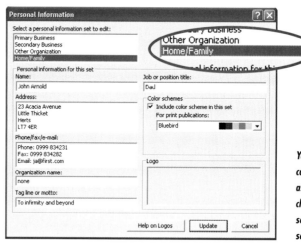

Your personal information can even include colour data as well as text. You can choose a different colour scheme for each of the four sets of personal information.

With Publisher's personal information sets, you can easily adapt elements of your document designs to suit your purpose, be it for business or pleasure.

Editing and using personal information

Publisher gives you four independent sets of personal information that you can choose from and adapt so that they suit different types of publications.

1 Start Publisher and open a blank document. Select Personal Information from the Edit menu.

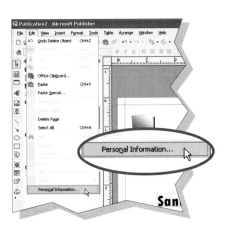

2 Depending on the publications you have already created with Publisher, the Personal Information dialog box may contain some data that you have been prompted to enter previously. By default, the Primary Business set is selected in the uppermost panel.

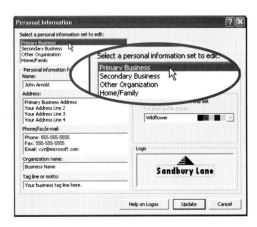

3 If you use Publisher for your business, work through each box and edit the placeholder information so that it matches your business details.

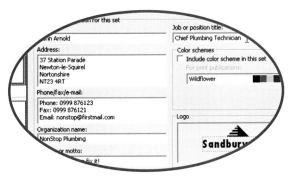

4 If you want to choose a preferred colour scheme, tick the Include color scheme in this set option and then select a suitable scheme from the drop-down list on the right. These will be used as the basis for your publications whenever you choose one of the templates you have created in Publisher. Finally, click on the Update button. Repeat the process for as many of the other three personal information sets as you wish to use.

5 Now click on the Insert menu and select Personal Information. Select one of the pieces of information. A text box appears in the document with the relevant text you entered into the Personal Information dialog box. You can position and format this text just as you would any other piece of text.

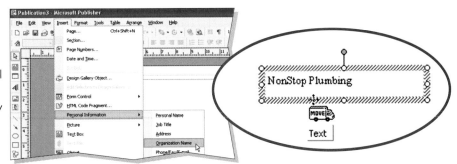

6 Try adding the other components. Using the Personal Information option instead of typing saves time and ensures that you never print documents with embarrassing spelling mistakes in these important items. If you want to add colour to the objects, you'll find that the colour scheme you chose in Step 4 is automatically selected in the Color Schemes Task Pane.

NONSTOP PLUMBING

Chief Plumbing Technician

If it drips, we can fix it!

n Arnold
tation Parade
on-le-Squirel
onshire
3 4RT

Phone: 0999 876123
Fax: 0999 876121
Email: nonstop@firstmail.com

PC TIPS

You'll notice that once you have added personal information, Publisher templates automatically pick up the details for documents you create. For example, a new postcard document will have the correct return address inserted without you having to lift a finger.

Hardware

Keeping it clean

Due to static electricity, your computer acts as a magnet for dust. It's important to keep it clean, not just for appearance, but to avoid malfunctions that can easily be caused by dirt and grime.

A computer attracts dust and, if neglected, this can prevent it from working properly.

Most computers are a dull grey that seems to be a very uninspired colour selection. There is a good reason for this seemingly boring choice, however. International regulations have stated that to limit eye strain the colour contrast between a monitor and its surrounding apparatus should be minimized.

However, because of this standard grey colouring, computers can look distinctly grimy unless they are kept clean. The effect is made even worse by the slightly textured surface of the plastic – again, it's designed to cut down reflections and reduce eye strain, but it also allows dirt to become engrained very easily.

Dust and grime on the computer not only look unpleasant, but can also do real harm. Excess dirt on the fan or power sockets, for instance, can sometimes cause components to fail, while the inner mechanisms of the mouse will not work effectively if dust gets trapped inside and so will hamper smooth movement.

● Grime prevention

You can clean the outer casing of the computer with an everyday household cleaner and a dust-free cloth, but the PC's monitor, keyboard and back of the system unit need rather more gentle treatment.

For the screen and keyboard, you should use a special anti-static spray that reduces static and repels dust. You can buy these sprays, designed for hi-fi and computer equipment, from most electrical dealers. A can of pressurized air is also good for cleaning inaccessible areas, but you need to take care not to deliver the blast of air too close to delicate electronic components.

It is also possible to buy a mini-vacuum cleaner for sucking out dirt from between the keyboard keys. These are available from most computer stores for around £10.

Disk drives also benefit from regular cleaning. The best method is to use a head-cleaning diskette with cleaning fluid once a week. A cleaning diskette is available from computer shops for around £5.

● Spill drill

It's very easy to spill tea, coffee and other liquids over the keyboard but they can be cleaned off with a special computer cleaning fluid, as long as the drips are easily accessible.

CLEANING YOUR MOUSE

Your mouse gets dirty at a faster rate than any other part of your computer, as it constantly rolls back and forth over the mouse mat, collecting dust. The mouse's internal parts, especially the rollers, need to be kept really clean if it is to continue working properly. This is done by simply removing the ball and scraping the grimy rollers with the head of a match.

Refer back to our guide (see Stage 1, page 93) for step-by-step tips on mouse maintenance.

Screen wipes

A particular problem with the screen is the build-up of static electricity. Its most obvious effect is that it attracts dust and makes the screen dirty very quickly. Since you look at the screen whenever you're working on the computer, it is worth getting into the habit of cleaning it regularly.

The easiest way to clean the screen is to use an anti-static, lint-free screen wipe. These are typically sold in packs of 100 for around £5 and are widely available in high-street electrical stores or through mail-order office and computer supplies companies.

It is possible to use a glass-cleaning fluid and a soft cloth rather than a specialist cleaner – but do not use any fluid that is not specifically sold for use on glass. If you have a flat screen monitor, make sure that you follow the manufacturer's recommendations for cleaning.

A longer-term way of dealing with screen dirt is to put a protective filter in front of the screen. Such screen filters are designed mainly to reduce glare and can also shield you from potentially harmful emissions, but they also reduce static electricity, so less dust is attracted to your screen. You will still have to clean your screen, but not quite so often.

Where there's smoke

Computer users who smoke risk the added danger of tobacco ash and smoke being drawn into the computer through the floppy disk drive (the cooling fans operating inside the computer suck air – and smoke – through the computer). So you should do everything you can to keep cigarettes away from your computer at all times.

Keep your machine clean

Try to clean your computer on a regular basis – don't just wait until it's really dirty. Here we show you a good cleaning routine to try.

1 Turn off your computer, making sure it is also switched off at the mains plug. If you use a spray while the computer is still on, you not only risk getting an electric shock, but you could also damage your computer.

2 Start on the monitor, using a special anti-static spray. Squirt a small burst on to a lint-free cloth and then immediately wipe it over the screen. This is safer than squirting the cleaner directly on to the screen because excess liquid might drip between the screen and the monitor casing, where it could do damage. Avoid using too much cleaner or you'll create smears.

3 Now start on the keyboard. You should use a mini-vacuum cleaner, if you have one, to suck out all of the dust and debris. Don't press down too hard between the keys unless your cleaner has a special narrow nozzle attachment. If any of the keys are very dirty, wipe them with a cloth or use a special keyboard fluid. Do not use any liquid other than special computer cleaning fluids.

4 Cleaning the casing of your computer is not such a delicate task: it can be cleaned much like any other appliance. To remove stubborn dirt from the casing, rub gently with a cloth.

WHAT NOT TO DO

NEVER use a general household cleaning liquid on the screen, keyboard or connecting slots. Household cleaners could damage circuitry and encourage static electricity.

NEVER use an alcohol-based fluid on the screen. The screen has an invisible coating that can be damaged by these cleaners.

NEVER clean anything while the power is still on.

NEVER place an ashtray or hold a cigarette just in front of your computer's floppy disk drive.

NEVER use a household duster to clean your computer as it will have gathered dirt from around the house. The static on the computer will attract dust from the duster, making the situation even worse.

NEVER try to push a duster, or anything else, into the inside of your computer.

NEVER get water or other liquids inside any part of your computer, as even small splashes can cause damage.

The soul of the machine

If the processor is the brain of your PC, then the BIOS is its soul – the basic built-in program without which the computer would remain a lifeless, inert piece of machinery.

A PC is a pretty useless machine without its Windows operating system, and its applications software, such as Word or Excel.

Together, these programs make your computer do the things you want it to do, but none of these programs existed on your PC when it was made. All of them (even Windows) come on CD-ROM or disk and have to be installed, either by you or by the manufacturer. Before this, however, the PC needs to have the ability to switch itself on in the first place and to know how to load up and deal with the software you install. This is where the essential BIOS comes in.

● What is the BIOS?

The name BIOS stands for Basic Input/Output System. It is called 'basic' because it determines what your PC can do without having to find and run programs from a disk. Although the BIOS is itself a program, it is not loaded from a disk but is installed on your PC during manufacture. It is normally written in to one or more ROM chips that are mounted on the computer's motherboard. Due to its in-built nature, software such as the BIOS is sometimes called 'firmware'.

The first, and fundamental, job of the BIOS is to carry out all the tasks that need to be done when you switch on your PC. Since your operating system and software are installed on your hard disk, they cannot start themselves but have to be fetched from the disk. It is the job of the BIOS to 'boot up' the operating system (meaning literally to 'pull itself up by its own bootstraps').

● Controlling the start-up

When you switch on your computer, the BIOS first performs a number of diagnostic operations, such as checking the memory. While it is doing this, you will notice numbers whizzing round on screen. It then initializes system components, such as graphics cards. This operation is called POST – Power-On Self Test.

Some BIOS chips are removable – the idea being that you can upgrade your BIOS by replacing it with a new chip. However, most modern PCs have BIOS chips that you can upgrade through software, so there's no need to open up the case and risk damaging delicate components.

BIOS MANUFACTURERS

When IBM made its first PC in the very early 1980s, it had its own proprietary BIOS, which was what made it an IBM, rather than any other kind of PC.

Anyone wishing to make an IBM-compatible PC (a 'clone') could obtain the operating system and applications software – but they could not buy an IBM BIOS. Nor could they simply find out how the program worked and copy it, since that would have been an infringement of intellectual copyright. So the cloners 'reverse engineered' it; they figured out how it did what it did, and then wrote their own software to do the same job. Not everybody got it right; many early clones were far from compatible and often crashed. Phoenix Technologies were among the first successful BIOS manufacturers and their BIOS is still widely used today. The other major supplier of BIOS chips is American Megatrends.

You may also see a series of plain text messages appear, one of which will tell you the manufacturer and version of the BIOS that is installed (see BIOS manufacturers box, opposite). The BIOS then 'calls' the operating system, and Windows takes control.

● Running operations

While getting your PC going is the first task of the BIOS, it is by no means its only one, for the BIOS remains a vital link between hardware and software in the computer at the most basic level. All the time the PC is switched on, the BIOS acts as the go-between for hardware, processor, operating system and applications. Whenever you press a key or save a file, for example, the BIOS is involved, either by dealing with device drivers that control your hardware and peripherals, or by interpreting commands known as 'interrupts'.

Interrupts are generated by various hardware activities, such as pressing a key or clicking the mouse, and are handled by a special chip called the interrupt controller. This tells the processor to stop what it is doing and attend to a command. In many cases – such as a key press – the BIOS will

contain specific instructions that are associated with this command. These instructions in the BIOS make the processor fetch the code representing the key press, transfer it to your applications software and then display the given character on-screen.

● Keeping up to date

Other types of hardware operation (especially those associated with peripherals, such as disk drives and graphics cards) are governed by device drivers. These are small pieces of program code designed to control a specific item of hardware.

Without device drivers, the BIOS would have to contain commands to deal with every piece of hardware you might wish to attach to your PC – a new printer, for example. Not only would this make the BIOS unmanageably large, but it would also result in the BIOS becoming out of date as soon as a new peripheral appeared on the market.

Indeed, some basic commands for handling peripherals are built into the BIOS. If the commands associated with a given peripheral are built in, then the BIOS sends the instructions directly to the device; if not, then it

gets the commands from the device driver and sends them on to the device. This means that any company which puts new equipment on sale has to provide a driver that loads onto your computer. The maker can then be confident that the BIOS will work with the new device.

ALTERING THE SETUP

Although the BIOS normally handles the start-up procedure automatically, you can interrupt the process and make some changes to the hardware configurations the BIOS uses. Usually this is done by pressing the [Del] key or one or more other keys, either alone or in combination. There will probably be a message on screen along the lines of 'Press DEL to enter SETUP' that will tell you the procedure.

The only reason people occasionally want to tinker with the BIOS settings are to change the hard disk settings – when the hard disk has been upgraded, for example – or to change the Power Management settings. These essential settings should be altered with extreme caution; you should leave all other settings to an expert, as it is very easy to damage your system by selecting the wrong ones.

Modern PCs use more integrated circuitry than PCs of a few years ago and some combine the BIOS with chips controlling other functions. This SMC chip contains circuitry from American Megatrends, who make BIOS chips and circuits.

Chip-making

The cleanest environment is required to make the world's smallest but most complex device – the computer chip.

The brains of your PC are provided by the many chips located inside it. The largest and most complex of these is the Central Processing Unit (CPU) – the microprocessor which is at the heart of all that your PC does. But there are many other chips: memory chips that store data; graphics chips that give you fabulous colour and three-dimensional images; sound chips that play a library of music; and many more. All these chips are produced by one of the most complex and painstaking manufacturing processes in the world.

There are, typically, more than 100 different steps in manufacturing a chip. All chips are made from semiconducting materials, the most widely used of which is silicon. This is the second most common element on the planet after oxygen. A semiconductor is a material that can be either a conductor or an isolator of electricity, depending on the way it is treated.

● Silicon wafers

First, silicon must be formed into a 'wafer' – a thin, round slice about 30cm in diameter – which will eventually hold hundreds of individual chips.

The wafer is created by heating purified silicon, which is derived from sand, until it is molten. A 'seed' (a small piece of solid silicon) is then placed on the hot liquid, which cools to form one large crystal ingot as the seed is pulled away from it. The ingot is then ground to a uniform diameter and cut into thin wafers using a diamond saw. Each wafer is ground smooth and then chemically polished until it is as smooth as a mirror. Afterwards, it is sent to the wafer fabrication facility – the heart of a chip factory.

It is here that the crucial steps for turning the silicon wafers into chips take place. These steps are carried out

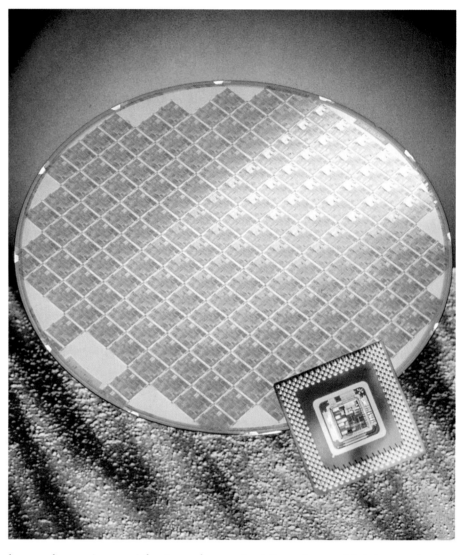

Round silicon wafers are polished mirror-smooth and then chemically treated before they have hundreds of chip circuits drawn upon their surfaces.

by people wearing special suits and filter masks to ensure that not a particle of human skin or a drop of sweat contaminates any stage of the manufacturing process. If even the tiniest atmospheric particle comes into contact with the wafers, it would destroy the processors. For this reason, the 'clean room' in a chip plant has an air-filtration system that leaves the atmosphere 10,000 times purer than in an operating theatre.

It can take from 10 to 30 days to carry out the various stages that the silicon wafers undergo in the fabrication room. The wafers are first chemically cleaned before they are exposed to pure oxygen to form a silicon dioxide film of uniform thickness on the surface.

● Making light work

The next, and most critical, stage is known as photolithography, in which the various layers of the chip are established and the integrated circuits are created. This stage of Photolithography is sometimes known as photo-masking, due to the masks that are applied to the wafer to protect one area of it while another is exposed to light.

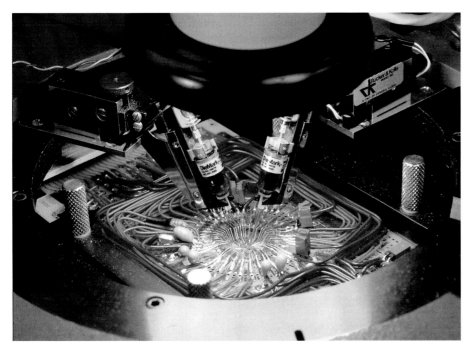

Each chip on the wafer undergoes thousands of diagnostic tests using computer-controlled machines like the one shown here.

The planning and finance required to prepare the way for chips is every bit as impressive as the feats of miniature and precise manufacture that are involved in making them. Microprocessor manufacture is one of the most expensive businesses in the modern world. It requires fortunes to be invested in both research and development and, if these elements are successful, in plant construction.

● New generations

Each new generation of PC chip is more complex and powerful than its predecessor, demanding vast new factories using the latest technologies to be built at ever increasing cost.

It is quite possible, if current trends continue, that at some point in the future chip makers will be unable to recoup the $4 billion or so it takes to build a new chip factory and make a profit as well. This is because they only have a brief amount of time before the new chip is superseded by an even newer one.

However, that time is still many years away, and by then it is more than likely that current research will have paid dividends by providing new ways to manufacture ever smaller and more powerful chips.

The wafer is placed in position by a photo-aligning machine and an intense beam of light is then projected onto the mask to engrave the circuits on the exposed areas. These etched areas are then treated to alter the electrical character of the silicon. Various layers on the wafer (which may be a mere 10 atoms thick) are then created by repetition of these processes and are held together by aluminium bonds to create the final microprocessors.

When the entire wafer is finished, each of the individual microprocessors on it is subjected to as many as 10,000 electrical tests per second; any elements failing these tests are marked with a drop of ink and are discarded when the diamond saw slices up the silicon wafer into separate chips.

A stage known as encapsulation follows as the chips are covered with a plastic protective coating and then fitted with the wires (narrower than a human hair) which are their electrical contact with the outside world. A final series of rigorous tests is carried out to ensure correct functioning under the real-world variables of temperature, humidity, vibration and so on, before the chips are packed in readiness for delivery.

WHO MAKES CHIPS?

Although it is the best-known manufacturer of PC chips, Intel has many competitors. It's quite possible that your PC is powered not with an Intel chip but by one produced by AMD. In addition, Motorola is a massive electronics company which produces many of the chips that power mobile phones, modems and other telecommunications devices.

Many of the world's large computer and electronics companies, notably IBM, Hitachi and Siemens Nixdorf, have established their own chip design and manufacturing facilities. They produce chips not just for their own computers, but increasingly for the wide range of devices that now require embedded processors to allow them to operate.

In addition to the market leaders, there is also a host of smaller companies who specialize in meeting the needs of narrower market segments, such as those who provide chips for weapons systems or satellite communication systems.

A technician, suited from head to toe, checks the logical functions of the wafer mounted in the tray on the right, just below the monitor.

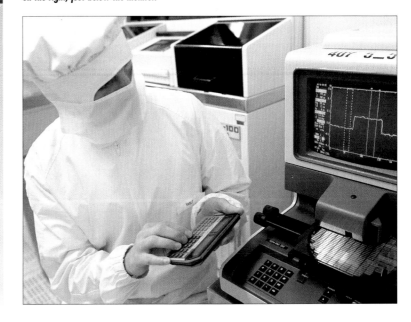

Cables and connectors

Different cable connector designs can be confusing with their myriad styles of pins and sockets, so let's take a closer look at them.

The many high-tech components of your PC are all connected via cables. These cables may look unimportant when they are compared to 2GHz processors and 80GB hard disks, but each cable has been designed and manufactured to very demanding standards.

Computer cables have an outer covering – which should never be tampered with – that holds a bundle of smaller wires which connect to pins or sockets at the end of the cable. The different designs help to ensure that data can be transferred quickly and without corruption as it passes along the cable.

● Male and female connections

Whether a wire ends in a pin or a socket depends on whether the connection at the end of the cable is male or female. A male connection is all pins, while a female connection is all sockets. If one end of the cable is different from the other, this indicates that one end connects to the PC and the other to the external hardware. Making a connection to a piece of hardware is a simple case of pushing the two together, as you would put a plug into a wall socket.

Two factors determine whether a connector will fit in a hardware socket and, subsequently, what it is used for. The first is the type of cable technology used. There are various standards (serial and PS/2, for example) and most are designed with a particular use in mind. Unlike much other PC hardware technology, cable connections have stayed pretty much

the same over the years, although a number of new technologies, such as USB, have recently appeared and are rapidly replacing the older ones.

The second differentiating factor with a cable is the number of pins or sockets it has. This can vary, since each cable is adapted for particular uses. Each pin, and its connecting wire, transfers certain types of information. There are two main sizes

of connector for each technology: the larger should have more than enough pins for most uses, while even the smaller one will have some pins that are not used.

● USB

The Universal Serial Bus (USB) is a standardized connector system designed to replace the array of serial and parallel ports and allow simple

Plugs and sockets allow digital data to be transferred between external devices and the PC's motherboard. They come in many shapes and sizes but some are more efficient than others.

attachment of PC peripherals (see Stage 4, pages 102–103). The USB connector itself uses a rectangular plug that fits a small slot.

There are many advantages to USB. For example, it is 'hot pluggable' (see Hot plugging box, below), it is much faster than most other types of PC connections, and you can run up to 127 separate devices on a single PC, either by daisy-chaining them next to each other, or by using a USB hub. Almost all modern desktop PCs are supplied with at least two USB sockets.

There are actually two types of USB device – versions 1 and 2 – but the connectors and cables look exactly the same. USB version 2 is much faster but the two versions work perfectly together.

● Serial port

The serial port is one of the oldest types of cable connection still in widespread use today. The two most common configurations for a serial port are 9-pin and 25-pin.

A serial port is slower than most other connections as it can transmit only one bit of data at a time – that is, one bit after another. Nowadays, serial ports are mainly used if you need to plug in an older, non-USB modem. In MS-DOS, serial ports are known as COM ports. If your computer has more than one serial port, they will be labelled COM1, COM2 and so on in Windows.

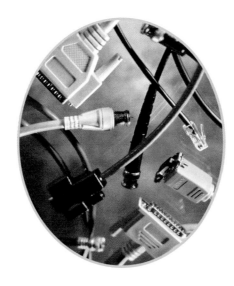

Screw in, plug in, clip in, rotate – there are many ways to connect a cable to a computer. USB rationalizes these different systems.

● Parallel port

The other stalwart of the PC cabling world is the parallel port. These are 25-pin connectors and today are used almost exclusively for connecting non-USB printers. As a result, they are often referred to as printer ports, or LPT1 in MS-DOS terminology.

● PS/2 port

The mouse and the keyboard usually have their own connection port and cable. The exceptions to this general rule are the small number of new PCs supplied with a keyboard and mouse that plug into USB sockets, and very old PCs that have a mouse that plugs into a serial port.

The PS/2 ports – colour coded to match up with the PS/2 plugs on the keyboard and mouse – each have six pins. This gives a clue to the encoding of data that goes on inside each device. For example, the keyboard has more than 100 keys but, to avoid the need for 100 or more connectors, it has some built-in intelligence to convert your key presses into

short codes, therefore enabling it to send them along fewer wires.

● IEEE 1394

This awkward jargon is the official name for what is sometimes called FireWire. Although they amount to the same thing, FireWire is an Apple trademark and other manufacturers cannot use the name. This connection provides the fastest data transfer yet between your PC and other IEEE 1394 devices, such as digital camcorders and external hard disks.

IEEE 1394 plugs and sockets have six connectors and share USB's hot-swapping benefits (see Hot plugging box, below). Few PCs have IEEE 1394 sockets yet, but they are likely to become increasingly popular. As more people buy digital camcorders and edit their videos on PC, so there is a greater need to find a fast way of transferring video to the PC's hard disk. You can add IEEE 1394 sockets by installing an expansion card.

● Other connections

The other external connections on your computer, apart from the power socket plug, include the connector between the monitor and the video card, almost always a 9- or 15-pin serial-type connection. In addition, there is the game port, a simple 15-pin serial connector installed as part of your sound card or as a separate (sometimes twin-socket) PC card.

A small number of older PCs may also feature a Small Computer System Interface (SCSI) socket. SCSI is a method of connecting devices in a daisy chain, often used for connecting scanners, Zip drives and external hard disks. The SCSI socket uses a large connector with dozens of individual connections. A SCSI socket is almost always on an expansion card as they were never a standard PC component.

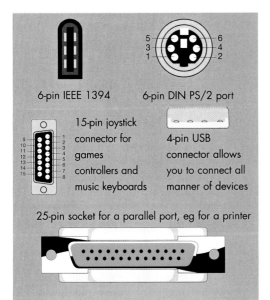

6-pin IEEE 1394   6-pin DIN PS/2 port

15-pin joystick connector for games controllers and music keyboards

4-pin USB connector allows you to connect all manner of devices

25-pin socket for a parallel port, eg for a printer

The illustration above shows what the most commonly used sockets at the back of your computer look like and what they are for.

HOT PLUGGING

Usually when you attach new hardware devices to the back of a PC, you have to restart the machine before the device is fully recognized by Windows. Hot plugging (sometimes called hot swapping) allows you to use the hardware immediately. There are two recently introduced external bus standards currently supporting hot plugging, namely Universal Serial Bus (USB) and IEEE 1394. Connections for these, particularly the former, have become commonplace on new PCs.

How buses work

Just as we need to have ways of communicating with a PC, so your computer components must have some means of 'talking' to each other. Most of the major internal system components communicate with each other using one or more 'buses'.

Buses in your computer have a major role in transporting information from one component to another.

A ll the components inside your computer – from its internal memory to the hard disk – need to be able to communicate with each other. They have to exchange electronic data constantly, and sometimes at very high speeds. For example, when a PC reads some data off the hard disk, it will also need to send the data to the memory. But to ensure there is no significant slowing down as you run a program, this operation has to happen very quickly.

● **Communication channels**
The part of the computer that makes all this possible is called a bus. Despite its name, a bus is just a channel, physically not much more than a collection of wires, through which information flows between three or more devices. Most of your PC's internal components, including the processor, memory, expansion cards and storage devices, talk to each other over one or more buses.

A bus has numerous access points to which you can attach extra devices, allowing them to communicate with all the other devices that are also connected. This is quite a common idea in the world of electronics; it's essentially how the phone line works in your house (no matter how many phone extensions you have, they're all connected to the same wire, which is

also a bus). Individual computers on a Local Area Network (LAN) are also connected in the same way, but in this case the bus is called the 'backbone'.

There are, in fact, a number of different buses in any PC, each one specializing in communications between different sorts of device. The basic type is the internal bus, which links the internal components to the processor and main memory. There will also be an 'expansion bus', used to connect any expansion cards and give them separate access to the processor and main memory.

Peripheral devices, such as scanners and printers, are always linked via an external bus (see External buses box, right), but ultra-fast connections are made via a local bus. This is a direct connection to the PC's processor and is used for any data, such as video, that must have especially high transfer speeds. It is the computer equivalent

EXTERNAL BUSES

An external bus connects your PC to external devices so the bus itself is partly outside the PC. The major development for PC owners in the 1990s was the adoption of the Universal Serial Bus as a means of connecting peripherals (see page 102).

USB is not only faster than a serial interface, it also guarantees a constant delivery rate of data. This is useful for streaming audio and video (video and sound files that are sent over the Internet and played as they arrive on your PC). USB is also a 'plug and play' interface – any USB-compatible hardware you plug in works straight away without needing to use extra software or a system restart.

Another advantage of USB is that it is used by both PCs and Macintosh computers. Peripherals such as printers can be attached to the USB ports on both types of computer – in the past, printer manufacturers had to design a printer for each type of computer.

of a motorway, compared to the slower B-road route which is taken by the standard internal bus.

● Bus width and speed

All types of bus consist of two parts: a data bus and an address bus. The data bus is the part responsible for physically transferring data through the bus and around the computer, while the address bus is concerned only with finding out where the information needs to go.

It is the address bus that actually determines how fast and effective a bus – and, ultimately, your PC – is. The 'wider' an address bus is, the more memory locations it can address at the same time, and the faster your machine will operate.

The 'width' of the address bus is a measure of how much data it can transfer at one time. This is where the whole notion of data 'bits' comes from. A 32-bit PC, for example, means that the bus can transmit 32 data elements simultaneously.

Whatever the width of the bus, it will not be effective unless software is written to take advantage of it. For example, Windows 95 was the first 32-bit version of Windows, so this was one of the main reasons for its increased speed over earlier versions.

● Bus developments

Like your processor, the bus has its own clock speed measured in MHz. The closer this speed is to that of the computer's main processor, the faster the whole system will run. The current

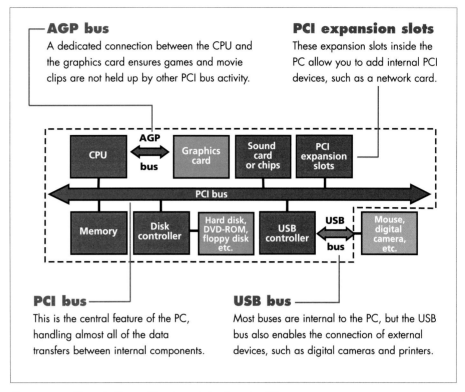

AGP bus
A dedicated connection between the CPU and the graphics card ensures games and movie clips are not held up by other PCI bus activity.

PCI expansion slots
These expansion slots inside the PC allow you to add internal PCI devices, such as a network card.

PCI bus
This is the central feature of the PC, handling almost all of the data transfers between internal components.

USB bus
Most buses are internal to the PC, but the USB bus also enables the connection of external devices, such as digital cameras and printers.

There are several buses inside your PC, each one designed to suit a different type of component, from the humble mouse to the ultra-fast graphics card.

bus standard is known as Peripheral Component Interconnect (PCI), which has been around in one form or another since 1993. Before this, the slower ISA bus was used, but has now been superseded by the PCI bus.

As Intel has introduced faster chips over the years, so PCI has had to speed up to match the higher processor power. This has led to the arrival of later standards, such as PCI-X, designed mainly for the server market, and projects such as InfiniBand, which is a new way of

connecting computers that's faster than the methods used today.

However fast (see Bandwidth box, below) or wide the bus has become, the task of displaying increasingly complex graphics has always depleted its resources. To deal with this, Intel developed the Accelerated Graphics Port (AGP), which takes the job of displaying 3D graphics away from the main bus. Since 1998, AGP has been standard on PCs and, because it's one of the most important buses on the PC, it's constantly being improved.

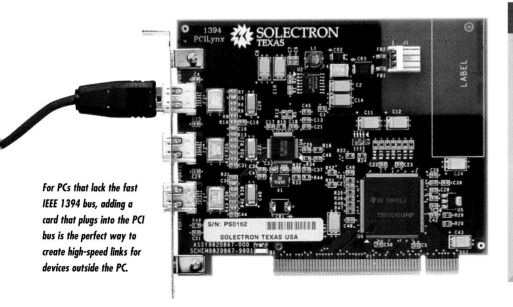

For PCs that lack the fast IEEE 1394 bus, adding a card that plugs into the PCI bus is the perfect way to create high-speed links for devices outside the PC.

BANDWIDTH

Bandwidth is the amount of data that can be transferred in a given time and it is a vital factor in the performance of a bus. This DTR (data transfer rate) is measured in megabytes per second (Mbps). The bus in an early PC of the mid-1980s ran at a meagre 2 to 8 Mbps; current PCI buses can manage around 266 Mbps. This performance boost was required because when Windows 3.0 arrived in 1990, PCs had to display screens full of images – not just a few hundred text characters. AGP's DTR is faster still, at 2.1 Gbps, to cope with the intensive job of processing and displaying 3D graphics.

PC Cards

PC adaptor cards are getting ever smaller, driven by the need to pack more power into the increasingly popular mobile phone and palm-top devices.

Notebook computer owners these days expect just as much from their systems as desktop owners do. In the same way that desktop owners can plug new cards into their PCI internal expansion slots, or plug external devices into USB sockets, so too can notebook users expand their systems with new hardware – the capability and performance of which belies its compact size. Thanks to the wonders of miniaturization, modems, network capability and even hard disk drives can now be crammed onto a card that is the same width and height as a credit card.

Since the early 1990s, these tiny add-ons have conformed to a series of standards under the blanket heading of PCMCIA (Personal Computer Memory Card International Association). Before then, add-ons were proprietary, with a good deal of variety – and incompatibility – existing between manufacturers. PCMCIA defined the physical size, power source, socket design and software of a notebook computer expansion card and, eventually, gave it its official name: the PC Card.

● Three types

As the name suggests, PCMCIA was originally a standard for memory cards (providing additional RAM), but it has evolved over the years to take in all manner of devices.

Notebook computers get much of their expansion capabilities from PC Cards. Network, Multimedia and even video capture devices are also supported by PC Cards.

There are two fundamental areas of development: changes to the form factor, or the physical size, of the card; and changes to the card's technical specifications. Form factor development resulted in three different sizes – namely Type I, Type II and Type III. Type I is the original 3.3mm-thick card. It is used mainly for memory cards, although other devices do exist. Type II boosted the thickness to 5mm, a common size for all kinds of card. Type III more than doubled the thickness to 10.5mm, and is used mainly for hard drives. All three cards have the same connector – or 'bus' – and so can be

plugged into the same slot, assuming there isn't a problem with thickness. For example, you can plug a Type I card into a Type II or Type III slot, but not the other way around.

● Increasing capabilities

As for the technical developments, PCMCIA Release 1.0 was the original version, designed for memory cards. Release 2.01 incorporated two standards: AIMS, which specified a more efficient way of storing and retrieving Multimedia and image files; and ATA, which specified how PC Cards could incorporate hard disks. The Card and Socket Services

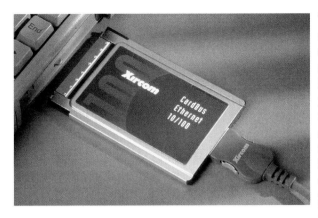

The Ethernet interface on a credit card-sized PC Card enables a notebook computer to link to desktop PCs and office networks.

specification in Release 2.1 improved communication between the cards and Windows. This made using PCMCIA cards easier – you needed to do much less manual setting up when adding a new PCMCIA card to the computer.

The next release added higher performance Multimedia with Direct Memory Access (DMA), plug-and-play, energy-saving compatibility and the major development of CardBus.

● CardBus

CardBus has reworked the PCMCIA bus structure (the card's information highway), making it compatible with 32-bit technology. In addition, it is also backwards-compatible in that it conforms to the standards in Releases 1 and 2. This means that notebook computers with CardBus can accept older cards. However, because CardBus PC Cards have a different connector, they will not plug into older sockets.

PCMCIA AND DESKTOPS

PC Card readers are available for desktop computers, either as an internal device that fits into the front of the PC like a floppy drive, or as an external one. You can then hot swap PC Cards (see Hot plugging box, page 103), just as you can with a laptop. The most useful application of this facility is probably the ability to transfer a hard drive to and from a notebook and desktop computers. The card readers are pretty cheap – typically under £100 – but you do have to pay the premium for the PC Cards themselves.

The introduction of plug-and-play technology has also made life easier for notebook owners. To install a PCMCIA card, you simply insert it into a free slot. The system then automatically recognizes the new hardware and installs the necessary drivers, perhaps asking you to insert a disc. Indeed, you can 'hot swap' PCMCIA cards: for example, you can take out a modem and plug in a new RAM card without shutting down the machine. The notebook system recognizes the change and alters the configuration.

● Smaller cards

PC Cards have been adapted for use in Personal Digital Assistants (PDAs), see page 110, and other hand-held devices by making them smaller. In 1998, the new Small PC Card was introduced, with the same standards as previous PC Cards, but about 42 per cent smaller. This means that PDAs driven by a cut-down version of Windows can have pretty much the same add-on capabilities as a regular notebook computer, for example Small PC Card modems and even Local Area Network (LAN) cards.

In 1998, the Miniature Card specification was also introduced for small flash memory cards. Designed for hand-held consumer electronic devices, from digital cameras to 'smart' digital phones, these cards are capable of accommodating 64MB or more of flash, ROM and D-RAM memory. Unfortunately for consumers, there is a rather confusing range of standards for these cards – including SmartMedia, CompactFlash, MultiMedia cards and Secure Digital cards. Although they are all broadly similar in operation, there is not yet an industry-wide standard so it is important to make sure you choose the right card for the right slot.

Despite the tiny size of this PC Card, there's a 5GB hard disk inside, allowing notebook users to upgrade their storage space or to transfer files to another computer with a PC Card slot.

● New developments

Proposed PCMCIA developments, both for hand-held devices and notebook computers, are set to extend PC Card technology to include the high-speed IEEE 1394 and Universal Serial Bus (USB) serial interfaces for PC Cards. This will then support such demanding uses as real-time video capture and notebook connections to fast networks. The original PC Card capabilities are now also filtering down to palm-top computers and should eventually appear in mobile phones.

This all means that, thanks to PC Cards, notebook computers can do most of the things that a desktop computer can – whether it's as part of a network, or performing high-capacity tasks such as video editing. On the down side, PC Cards tend to cost a bit more and any new technology might take a little longer to be incorporated into them. On the up side, it isn't necessary to shut down your PC to install them and they are becoming increasingly easy to use – plus they add necessary additional capabilities for those who are on the move.

BUYING PC CARDS

The PC Card specification is very flexible and PC Cards can add many useful capabilities to your notebook. However, the PC Card market is relatively small, and many computer dealers only stock the more popular devices, such as memory cards and hard disks. For a wider choice, visit an online dealer; you'll find cards for adding all sorts of devices, from a second monitor to a home PC network.

Notebook computers

Today's notebook PCs let you travel in style with powerful processors and lots of storage space – if you are happy to pay the price. If you need to compute on the move, a notebook PC could be just what you require.

Not long ago, notebook computers were little more than travelling office companions, limited by poor displays, slow processors and small hard drives. You could work on them when out and about, but you needed a desktop computer back at base for your main computing power. However, that's all changed now, as modern notebooks offer impressive portable power at a reasonable cost.

● A powerful little package
A typical notebook computer is just a little larger than this book and about three to four centimetres thick. But, as there's so much power packed inside, the notebooks can be quite heavy – between two and four kilos.

Notebooks are great if you're often on the move, but also take up less desk space at home.

You really can take a powerful PC, such as the IBM ThinkPad X (right), almost anywhere.

Open up its lid and the keyboard and screen are visible. The disk drives are usually placed on the sides of the unit, with the power socket at the back. Squeezing all the elements of a modern Multimedia computer – processor, memory, hard drive, CD-ROM drive, floppy disk drive and more – into such a small box can cause problems and sometimes there just isn't room for all the components. Very small notebook computers often forgo a CD-ROM drive, while others have a special compartment which can take either a floppy disk or CD-ROM drive, letting you alternate between the two as necessary.

Unlike pocket computers (see Stage 4, pages 110–111), a notebook PC runs the same Windows software as a desktop PC – not a cut-down version. These are true computers, running real applications in a full Windows environment.

● To suit all pockets
Today, you could spend over £2,000 on a top-of-the-range notebook featuring an ultra-fast processor, DVD drive, modem, hard drive, plenty of memory and a large full-colour screen. Such a computer will almost match your desktop computer for speed and capabilities. However, you needn't spend that much. A basic notebook can cost as little as £800. These computers usually have less memory, slower processors and smaller, lower-quality screens than the more expensive models.

In recent years the display has been the focus of much improvement in notebooks. Screens use a special colour variant of the LCD (liquid crystal display) that you find on digital watches. They have become both larger and their resolution sharper, making them a lot easier to read; the best are even suitable for working with graphics.

Most notebooks will also include sound cards and tiny speakers built into their casing. The sound quality does remain limited by the small size of the equipment, although the speakers are surprisingly effective.

Mouse alternatives

While a mouse would hinder the portability of a notebook, a Windows computer requires some type of mouse substitute to allow you to click on icons, use pull-down menus and highlight text. Notebooks use one of three different approaches.

The first is the touchpad – a small, rectangular panel positioned beneath the keyboard. As you move your finger across the touchpad, it senses your finger's position and makes the mouse pointer follow the same movements. Two small buttons near the touchpad function as the left and right mouse buttons.

Some computers use a miniature trackball, similar to the types you can buy as mouse replacements for your desktop computer. As you roll the ball, the mouse pointer moves.

Other computers use a tiny rubber stalk placed between the B, G and H keys (above right). It is very sensitive, translating the pressure from your finger into pointer movement.

Buying a notebook

When looking at the magazine adverts, take a note of the actual weight of the new notebook computers on offer.

Toshiba notebooks have a tiny, but easy-to-use stalk to replace the desktop mouse.

While the notebook itself can weigh just a couple of kilos, the actual weight with all accessories can soon add up to a lot more once you include the notebook's mains adaptor, spare battery and any of the extra plug-in devices.

To select a notebook that best suits your needs, you obviously have to ask all the usual questions that you would ask when choosing a desktop PC: Which software do you need to run? What are the memory and processor requirements? Is this notebook to be your only PC or will it be a second computer, only to be used for computing on the move?

If you already have a desktop computer, you might find that you can do without a CD-ROM drive in your notebook computer. It is also possible that you could make do with a slightly less powerful machine if you have plenty of computing power back at home for working with Multimedia computing and graphics.

A more personal preference will be which type of pointer device to choose. It isn't possible to change your notebook to use a different method, so try them all out in the

NOTEBOOK ACCESSORIES

The notebook computer's performance can be enhanced by adding extra accessories that might not be included in the basic model. These include:

Extra battery packs

All notebook computers have special programs that allow you to save battery power, but the most effective way of increasing your working time is to carry a second battery pack – about the size and weight of a typical mobile phone.

PC Cards

Notebook computers have special slots which accept tiny add-on devices. These devices, called PC Cards (see pages 106–107), are a standard shape. If your notebook doesn't have a built-in modem, you can add a PC Card modem.

CD- or DVD-ROM drive

If your notebook doesn't have a CD- or DVD-ROM drive, you can buy a special add-on version. These devices usually connect via the notebook computer's printer port (simple, but slow), or use a PC Card (faster, but more expensive).

Carrying cases

These not only keep your notebook free from dust and grime, but also provide storage for your accessories.

computer shop before you make your choice. If you don't feel comfortable with any of the options available, you can connect a normal desktop mouse.

Running on batteries

Finally, consider how much time you will spend using the notebook's battery power or running it while it is plugged into the mains electricity. All notebooks use rechargeable battery packs but they differ widely in the amount of power they consume. You can usually expect between two and four hours of battery life, so investing in a second battery will reduce the problem of running out of power.

Display

The LCD colour display has improved in recent years and the very best screens are a match for desktop computer monitors of similar size.

Keyboard

The keys are more cramped than on a desktop keyboard, but are still fine for most home users.

Connection sockets

Notebooks include almost all the connection sockets of the desktop computer, so you can plug in a printer, mouse or even a larger desktop monitor.

Drives

Most notebooks have both floppy disk and hard disk drives. Many also have a CD-ROM drive. Some of the smallest notebooks use an external floppy drive.

Battery

All notebooks have a built-in battery that provides enough power for up to four hours of computing without using mains electricity.

Pointing device

On this notebook PC a touchpad is used instead of a mouse.

Connecting handheld computers

By combining a handheld computer with a desktop computer, you can work while you're on the move and then edit and print your documents on your desktop PC when you get back to base.

Handheld computers, or Personal Digital Assistants (PDAs), can be very useful for computing on the move (see Stage 4, pages 110–111). Small and light enough to slip into a coat pocket, a handheld computer allows you to keep schedules and diaries up to date and lets you write notes and letters, store phone numbers and addresses, and even carry out spreadsheet calculations, wherever you happen to be.

● Connecting to a desktop computer

While a handheld computer is ideal for use on the move, you will probably need a desktop computer to print out documents. Portable printers are available, but few people can justify the extra cost or inconvenience. By connecting the handheld computer to your main PC, however, you can then use your standard printer.

A handheld computer has limited storage capacity – perhaps just 16–64MB – compared to the huge size of your desktop PC's hard disk. You can therefore transfer files from your handheld computer over to your desktop PC and save space on your handheld computer, while also providing a useful back-up.

You will probably also want to transfer files so that you can tidy up work that you started while on the move. The information you enter on your handheld computer while you're out and about is more likely to be in note form than a finished document. It's therefore useful to transfer a word processor document created roughly on your handheld computer to Microsoft Word for finalizing and formatting before printing it out (see File conversion formats box, right).

● Connection extras

Suppliers of handheld computers make the business of connecting to your desktop computer as simple and painless as possible. Many handheld computers include the software and cable in the price, and some handheld computers come with a desktop cradle so that connecting the two machines is just a matter of sliding the handheld into the cradle.

You can make your handheld and desktop computers work hand in hand by linking them up.

FILE CONVERSION FORMATS

In addition to the physical connection between handheld and desktop computers, it's important to think about software and document compatibility. Handheld computers often use different programs to their desktop companions and you should bear this in mind when choosing a handheld computer.

However, the most popular programs on desktop computers are Microsoft Word and Excel and most handheld computers can save your documents in a format that Word and Excel can use directly. The file transfer software takes care of any conversion that's needed and the options let you choose different formats if you don't use Word or Excel.

Synchronizing data on a handheld computer with a desktop PC

You can create files on your handheld computer and then transfer them to your desktop PC for finalizing.

FOR THIS example, we've used a Palm Tungsten T to show how a typical handheld computer communicates with a desktop PC. The principle is that the Palm's HotSync software automatically takes care of updating the data so that you can be sure you're always working on the right files. Most other handheld computers have similar features. There may be some differences in the menus and options, but the same general process applies.

1 Before you can synchronize the two computers, you need to install the software that came on the handheld computer on your PC. Insert the CD into the PC's CD-ROM drive and follow the on-screen instructions that appear.

2 At the end of the set-up process, you'll see one or more new icons on your PC's Desktop. In the case of the Palm Tungsten T, there's also a HotSync icon within the Notification area at the right of the Windows Taskbar.

3 The first step is to synchronize the two computers for the first time. With the Tungsten T, you do this by sliding the handheld into its desktop cradle and clicking on the HotSync button on the cradle. In an instant, a progress window appears on your desktop PC and shows the two devices communicating.

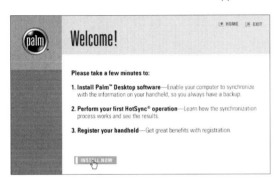

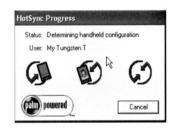

4 When synchronization is complete you can launch the Palm Desktop software by double-clicking on its icon on the PC. You'll see the information stored on the handheld. What you see depends on how much you have used your handheld. In this example, where the handheld is new, there are very few items.

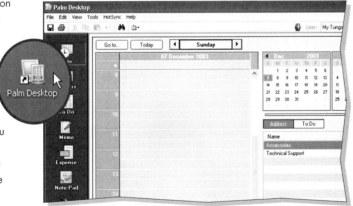

PC TIPS

Synchronizing PCs

In addition to transferring data between computers, you can also transfer new software. Use your desktop PC to visit the Web site of your handheld's manufacturer. Look for a Software download section to see if there are any useful or fun programs. If there's anything you like the look of, download it to your PC and then transfer the program to your handheld computer.

5 Now you can disconnect the handheld from the PC and use It as a portable computer, typing notes and entering information using its mini-programs. When you return to your PC, you can resynchronize the two sets of data. Reconnect the computers and start the HotSync process again.

6 Open the PC software once more. This time you'll see that the Information you have added to the handheld since the last synchronization now appears. In this example, there are two new contacts, and also a voice memo that we can now play via our desktop PC's speakers.

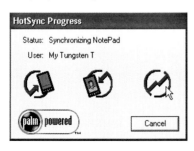

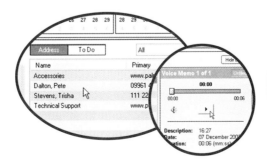

Home Learning & Leisure

WAP – the new Web?

The latest technology is now available on a mobile phone near you. But it's only the start of the revolution to enable Internet access from a huge range of miniature portable devices.

The traditional way of accessing the Internet is via a PC connected to a fixed telephone line. Your modem dials your ISP and when the connection is made you can check your email or browse through the millions of information sources on the Web. While effective, this method is beginning to look cumbersome when you consider the explosive growth in mobile phone usage. WAP (Wireless Application Protocol) could be the answer when you're on the hoof: it allows you to connect to the Internet via your mobile phone, giving you access to email and browsing functions at any time.

Even before WAP, mobile phones had some capability for data transmission. In 2002, some 186 billion mobile phone text messages were sent in Western Europe alone via the Short Message System (SMS). However, although popular, SMS is very limited – it is only capable of sending and receiving messages of up to 160 characters.

● Mobile browser

WAP, on the other hand, can give you much of the power of your PC's Internet browser on your mobile. It uses special software and a cut-down version of the Internet mark-up language HTML, known as WML (Wireless Mark-up Language). It is able to deliver many services that closely resemble those you are familiar with receiving from Web sites, directly onto your computer.

Although they are very similar, these services cannot be exactly the same as on your PC, largely because of the limited screen size and processing power of a mobile phone. Also, WAP phones on standard data connections have to make do with a relatively slow data speed of 9.6Kbps compared to a desktop modem's 56Kbps.

● Mini Web pages

WML is a way of providing special Web content to suit small screens. The first obvious difference in viewing Web pages on a WAP phone rather

Motorola has designed a prototype wrist phone that could be the shape of things to come. With built-in WAP, you'll be able to make voice calls and browse the Web.

WHAT IT MEANS

WAP

Wireless Application Protocol is a de facto standard agreed by the leading mobile phone manufacturers – principally Nokia, Motorola and Ericsson. It specifies how to use current Internet and telecoms technologies to allow you to browse cut-down versions of Internet sites and services on mobile telephones and handheld computers.

than on a PC is that the mouse operations are replaced by special buttons or screen icons, allowing you to scroll through the information on offer. There are also very few graphics with WAP content – they are simply too time-consuming to deliver. WAP-enabled mobile phones look no different from ordinary mobile phones, although a few do have larger screens.

● Getting connected

To get WAP content on your WAP phone you have to log on to special WAP Web sites. All the major operators, such as O2, Vodafone, Orange and T-Mobile, have developed special sites to provide their own or others' WAP content. You simply dial the special number that your service provider supplies.

Once you have established the connection, the process is very similar to using the Web on your PC: you click on links to move around and you can bookmark favourite sites for easier access. The costs are the same as making any other mobile call, but the phone companies are, of course, banking on you making more calls and staying on line much longer.

● Instant information

So what can you do with a WAP phone? Full email services on the move are an obvious advantage, but the service and content providers want to supply more complex services. Instant news information wherever you are is one of the main priorities, whatever your interests might be. Football fans, for example, can get their team's results over the phone.

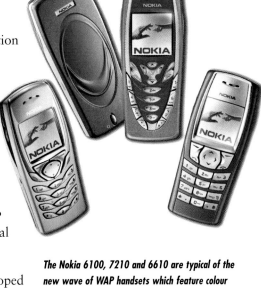

The Nokia 6100, 7210 and 6610 are typical of the new wave of WAP handsets which feature colour screens and high-speed data transmission for a slicker WAP experience.

● Online banking and more

Services such as online banking are already in place, while share-trading fanatics can get the latest prices and do deals when on the move. You can also check the weather forecast and even find out if your train is delayed. You can also buy goods online via your WAP phone. Using a WAP-accessible travel guide, you could find and book a cinema or restaurant wherever you happen to be. And, as WAP gets faster with better data communications (see Beyond WAP box, right), the possibilities for mobile commerce, or 'm-commerce', become much more exciting.

● The future of WAP

When WAP first appeared, it gained a poor reputation for unreliability and sluggish performance. Plain text was also disappointing when you were used to the lively colour and animation of full Web pages.

All these aspects have seen a lot of improvement in recent years, however. Faster data connections (see Beyond WAP box, below) offered by

WAP isn't the only way to access the Web from a pocketable device. Handspring's Treo 300 is a phone and organiser in one, with a screen big enough to load standard HTML Web pages, albeit in a miniaturised format.

the networks have helped enormously, as have colour screens and improved support for on-screen graphics. Soon you will be able to use your mobile phone to download and pay for digital music – and play it through headphones on the same phone. You might also be able to pay to watch video clips of football teams in action, rather than just finding out the score.

Whether these various developments are 'liberating' is a matter of personal taste, but the Internet is certainly expanding into all areas of life.

WHAT IT MEANS

GSM

GSM stands for 'Global System for Mobile communication', which is an international standard for the wireless technology that makes mobile phones work. The abilities to transmit voice, data, and SMS are all part of the GSM standard. GSM is now employed by nearly all mobile phone network operators throughout the world, with the exception of Japan and parts of the USA.

BEYOND WAP

WAP itself was just the first step in a three-stage process that is currently revolutionising mobile Internet access. The main improvements in the next two stages are in speed of delivery and this is already in full flow with General Packet Radio Services (GPRS), a wireless data transmission technology which increases the connection speed from standard GSM's 9.6Kbps to as much as 115.2Kbps – three times faster than even a fixed-line 56Kbps PC modem. Although the speed is too variable to make live video a practical application, it has helped trigger the current craze in photo messaging with camera phones.

The third generation of improvement is still under development, and often referred to generically as '3G'. No single standard has emerged yet, although a likely contender is UMTS (Universal Mobile Telecoms Services). This is a broadband system theoretically capable of a connection speed of 2,000Kbps per second.

Voice recognition

Once a favourite fantasy of science fiction, voice-recognition technology is now a reality. In the near future, it's set to play an increasing role in the way you control your computer.

It was only in the latter half of the 1990s that voice-recognition software for the home PC user became a realistic prospect. This breakthrough was due to rapid improvements in voice-recognition techniques and the increasing speed and power of PCs themselves.

Early programs were limited and frustrating: they worked quite slowly and had a relatively small vocabulary of words they could recognize, which meant that any dictation would result in masses of errors that you had to correct manually. Now the software seems to have come of age. Both ViaVoice (from IBM) and Dragon NaturallySpeaking (from ScanSoft) deliver voice recognition that is easy to use, fast and virtually free of errors – with recognition rates of 90 per cent and higher just a short while after installing the program.

● Continuous speech

The main improvement has been the move to continuous speech recognition, rather than discrete recognition. In the older form you had to speak slowly in a staccato fashion so that the program had enough time to work out each word or short phrase. Continuous recognition, however, allows you to speak in a normal voice at a normal pace and with all the usual pauses, which is clearly easier for the user.

There are other improvements, too. Early speech-recognition programs had a basic vocabulary – words they would recognize without being taught

– of 30,000 or less. Both ViaVoice and NaturallySpeaking offer 150,000-plus words on installation, and can be taught to recognize more than 50,000 additional words. The other major development is that speech recognition is no longer simply used for dictating documents. While dictation remains the main use, these programs have now been developed so that you can give Windows commands or surf the Net by voice. So, instead of using the mouse or keyboard, you could simply say 'Open a new Excel document' or 'Go to yahoo.co.uk'.

● Making a start

However, before you rush out and buy a voice-recognition program, consider first if you have a suitable PC. These programs require large amounts of RAM and fast processors – do not be tempted if you have anything less than 64MB of RAM and a 400MHz Pentium processor.

Even those specifications are really a bare minimum – 128MB of RAM and a 600MHz processor will make the software work much faster and therefore easier to use.

You will also need a sound card and a microphone. Both ViaVoice and NaturallySpeaking come with comfortable, quality microphone headsets; you simply plug these into the sockets on the sound card.

● Installation

Installing a voice-recognition program can seem a bit of a chore compared to other categories of software; this is because you not only have to transfer the program to your hard disk, you also have to spend time calibrating the microphone and audio levels. Allow around an hour to complete the process and practise.

Train your computer to recognize your voice and it will obediently follow all your orders.

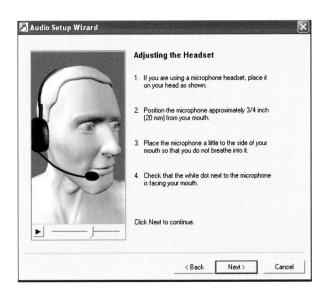

Setting up your microphone headset properly is important if you want optimum voice quality. Both ViaVoice and NaturallySpeaking give good advice on how to do this. ViaVoice (shown here) shows you a computer-generated model to follow.

Once you've 'trained' the software, simply open up the word processor and begin dictating. Then, as here with ViaVoice, just highlight and correct any mistakes that have been made so that the software will get it right the next time.

The practice time is crucial if you want to get the most out of your investment. The optimum set-up of your microphone system is also vital as you need to ensure the mouthpiece is in just the right position. You must then calibrate the audio settings to take into account the qualities of your voice, together with any background noise – although it's obviously best if you can choose somewhere that is usually fairly quiet.

Next, there is the task of training the software to recognize the words you speak – everyone's voice is unique and English has a wide variety of regional accents. This is where the processes called General Training (in NaturallySpeaking) and Creating a Personal Voice Model (in ViaVoice)

come in. Both programs use a very similar Wizard-driven set-up procedure, which can take up to 30 minutes. If you want to get the best out of your voice recognition software, you will need to follow this procedure carefully.

You have to read a lengthy passage of text in your normal dictation voice. The program absorbs the information, stopping you and prompting you to repeat words it has not understood clearly. By the time you finish the process you should be able to use the software, with a good-to-high recognition score.

Both programs are supplied with word-processing packages: SpeakPad with ViaVoice and DragonPad with NaturallySpeaking. When you launch the program, the relevant word processor window opens. Just activate the microphone and start dictating. You can format and lay out your text as easily as when using the keyboard: you simply issue the appropriate command, such as 'new paragraph' or 'open bracket/close brackets', and your commands will be carried out on screen.

Both programs allow dictation into any Windows program – although you might find that this is a slower method than in their own word-processor packages.

● **Continuous education**
Of course the software does make mistakes but these programs never stop learning. As mistakes are made you can correct them in drop-down windows, adding single words or whole phrases that will be recognized next time. For vocabulary building, you can teach the software many new words in one sitting; this is handy if you use any kind of specialized, technical or professional vocabulary, as in medicine and law, two fields where voice recognition has long been in widespread use.

CONTACT POINTS

Dragon NaturallySpeaking Essentials
Price: £46.99*
Dragon NaturallySpeaking Standard Edition
Price: £93.99*
Dragon NaturallySpeaking Preferred
Price: £149.99*
ScanSoft
Tel: 0118 963 7464
www.scansoft.co.uk

IBM ViaVoice Standard Edition
Price: £39.99*
IBM ViaVoice Pro USB Edition
Price: £95.99*
IBM
Tel: 01475 892 000
www.ibm.com/uk   *UK prices

The training process in Dragon NaturallySpeaking requires you to read a lengthy passage of text (thankfully in small chunks) so that the software can get used to your voice.

Discovering databases

Databases can be complex and powerful data-handling systems used by huge businesses, or they can be as simple as a family address book. Whatever the case, knowing what they can do is the first step to using these very handy programs.

A computerized database is like a manual card index, with one record equivalent to one card. Filing, sorting and identifying information by different fields is made so much easier when you ask a computerized database to do it.

How many databases do you use in the course of a normal day? Think about a phone directory, your address book or bank statement, TV listings, a cookbook and a train timetable – they're all databases.

The term 'database' sounds complicated and technical, but a database is simply a collection of information that is organized in a particular way. A database program (sometimes called a 'database manager') offers much more than that, however. It doesn't just store information for you – it lets you organize, analyse, access and generally use the information in several useful ways.

For example, a database will let you find particular information quickly. Tell the computer to search for a specific name or group of words and it will come back with a list of

items (records) that match. This might be useful when you are looking for a single record in the database – a CD from your audio collection, for example.

● **Selecting data**
More usefully, you can extract a selection of records, or 'subset', from the full database. So you could list everyone in your contacts database who has a Liverpool address by searching for 'Liverpool'. Or you could create a list of videos with a 'PG' (Parental Guidance) rating.

You can usually set up your first database simply by choosing a ready-to-go design from a set of templates. These will have all the fields normally needed by the task, and you can add or delete fields to customize the design.

The other really useful thing about databases is that information can be listed easily in different ways for different purposes. If you want to access your personal contacts, it makes sense to organize the database alphabetically by surname. For business purposes, however, you might find that it is much more useful to have the contact information arranged alphabetically by the name of the company.

If you're travelling around, it could be handy to have the names and addresses listed by city so you can see who's based in the city you're visiting. You could also get the database to output address labels sorted by postcode (useful in some countries where postal authorities give a discount for handling pre-sorted mail). None of this affects the basic data; it just provides other ways of viewing the database information.

● **Reporting**

Another very significant feature of databases is reporting. Information you have pulled out and organized can be presented to suit your needs – you don't always have to live with the database's standard way of presenting information on screen. In this sense, a 'report' isn't necessarily a long formal document: it simply means 'something that can be displayed or printed'.

One example might be a mailing label. You can select names from the database for a mailshot, and then check through your list in an easy-to-read, spreadsheet-style table with one record per row. Your mailing label obviously can't look like that, but a label 'report' could take the required information from each record, format it with appropriate punctuation and use a printable layout that fits the dimensions of a sticky label sheet for your printer.

Yet another advantage is the way databases can be used to produce new information. For example, let's say you have an expenses database into which you copy information from your bank and credit card statements, together with details of your other outgoings, such as the mortgage and any loan repayments. Using a database, you can easily devise a report that summarized how much money you are spending each month,

There are plenty of programs that will help you create your own databases from scratch. Some database managers allow you to include fields that are automatically calculated for you, such as the 'Date Created' and the 'Number of Servings' fields in this FileMakerPro example.

how the spending splits between regular commitments and occasional outlays, how this month's outgoings compare to last month's or to your average monthly expenditure, and so on.

● **How databases work**

Databases store information as records. A record is a collection of information about a single item arranged under headings, called fields. In an address book, each name and address entry is one record made up of separate fields for first name, surname, company name, address, town, phone number and so forth.

Most databases come with some predesigned layouts, so you can get started quickly by creating an empty database that uses one of these templates. The preset fields will appear on the screen enabling you to start entering the information straight away.

You'll be able to change this design, adding and removing fields from the layout to suit your own requirements. It is also possible to design and

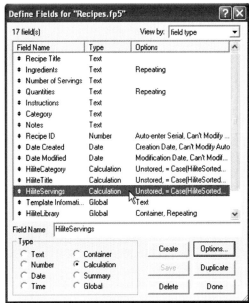

create your own database layout from scratch, although this can be quite a complicated process.

● **One step beyond**

With practice, some databases can be used to perform quite complex tasks, with macros and other tools doing a lot of the hard work for you automatically.

The most important thing is not to be intimidated by database managers such as FileMaker Pro or Microsoft Access – they are really quite easy to use and you could soon find that the versatility and power of these programs is surprisingly useful.

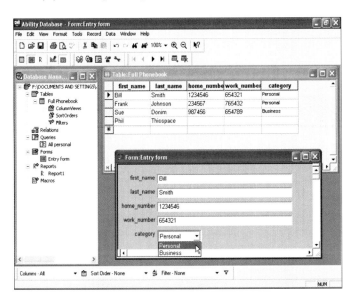

With most databases the basic structure is a spreadsheet-style table. In the Ability Database example above, each row is a single record and each column is a field in the record. Or, if you prefer, data can be entered using a cardfile-type form instead.

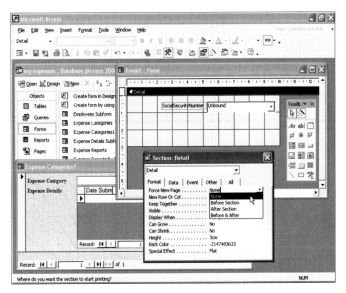

Modern database packages allow you to customise the appearance of forms and reports. Microsoft Access, shown above, even provides a form designer which works like a graphics program, but also has the ability to 'draw' pop-up lists and special fields.

The British Isles

With a Multimedia computer you can travel the length and breadth of the British Isles, learning about the history, people and places that make up this fascinating and diverse part of the world.

The virtual world of Multimedia offers both the armchair tourist and the serious geography student an entertaining way of discovering a huge amount of information about the world.

Learning about a place from a PC screen is not, of course, the same as going there and experiencing it for yourself, but you could spend many months travelling the British Isles and still not discover all the interesting things on offer.

The history of these islands is crowded with incidents and personalities, wars and great social changes. Then, of course, there is the geography, which is extremely diverse, ranging from the rugged mountains found in northern and western parts, to the gentle meadows and flatlands of the south and east. Finally, the cultural and architectural heritage of the islands – from Shakespeare to soap opera – is incredibly rich and fascinating.

Today you can find all the information you might need about the British Isles in a range of CD-ROMs, each of which makes good use of the sound, vision and interactivity that Multimedia offers.

● **Mapping it out**

The *Ordnance Survey Interactive Atlas of Great Britain* is not specifically a tourist or culture guide. As the name implies, it's a CD-ROM atlas of the country, but with so many Multimedia enhancements that it becomes much more than just that. This CD-ROM is great for both the serious geographer and the general user. The atlas on the CD-ROM displays maps in a range of scales, from the large 1:250,000 (2.5km to 1cm) down to the detail of 1:25,000 (250m to 1cm). As you'd expect from the Ordnance Survey – Britain's national cartographers for the past 300 years – landscape details and man-made features are all presented clearly and attractively. It's also

possible to adapt the on-screen view. So, for example, if you're interested in the physical geography of an area, such as its hills, valleys and rivers, you can turn off other features, such as roads and settlements, providing a clear view of the terrain.

● **Media map features**

The main map of the British Isles contains more than 300 Multimedia map pins (see inset, below) marking places of interest; click on one and you will see a photograph and a description. These locations range from physical features, such as Snowdon or Ben Nevis, to tourist and cultural spots, such as Chatsworth and Stonehenge. This CD-ROM also contains a glossary of geographical and geological terms and six learning modules on the subject of map skills. You can learn about scale and distance, longitude and latitude, grid references and so on.

Each module introduces the concepts clearly and contains

AA Where To Go in Britain and Ireland *gives a brief description and picture of each location, such as Castle Campbell (left). The Ordnance Survey Interactive Atlas of Great Britain (above) includes Multimedia map pins (inset), which provide detailed information when clicked on.*

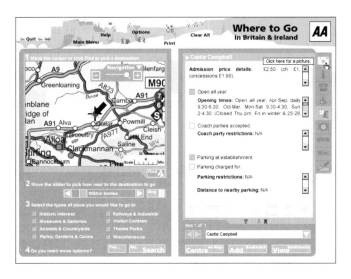

In AA Where To Go in Britain and Ireland, clear maps give detailed information on the location of tourist features that are covered on the CD-ROM.

Queen Elizabeth I is just one of the 2,800 biographies of significant people you can view in the Who section of AA Interactive Encyclopedia of Britain and Ireland.

practice exercises. These form an excellent introduction to using maps and are of particular value to geography students.

● Tripper's delight

The *AA Where To Go in Britain and Ireland* CD is a straightforward and practical directory that any potential day tripper will find useful. It lists 2,600 places of interest, giving descriptions, opening times, prices, locations and directions. It also includes maps you can print out and take on your travels.

Many of the attractions include photographs or video footage, and you can search by type (gardens, theme parks, castles) or by area. With all this information in one handy CD-ROM, you'll find plenty of ideas for trips out.

● Interactive Britain and Ireland

More ambitious in scope is the *AA Interactive Encyclopedia of Britain and Ireland,* an informative and thoroughly entertaining CD-ROM. It's slick, packed with facts and contains a great deal of video and audio material, in addition to the usual photography and text.

This CD-ROM is made up of four main sections: Who, What, Where and When, all of which are full of detail about the British Isles. For example, the Where section takes you to 'Britain's 10,000 most interesting places', each one offering a description and many of which are accompanied by an illustration. To focus your search you can select categories, such as Civil War, TV or Mysteries. If you select TV, you'll be able to see a multitude of locations used in the filming of popular television series.

If you're keen on exploring the towns and villages of the UK, then the *AA Interactive Encyclopedia of Britain and Ireland* is a great place to start planning your route around this rich and varied nation.

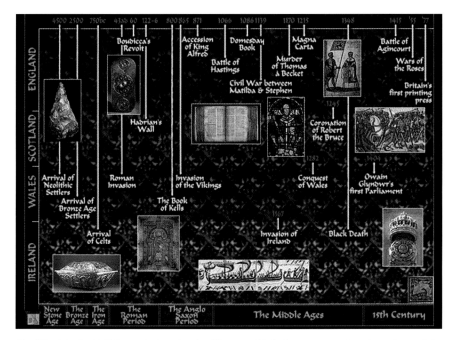

The 'When' timeline in AA Interactive Encyclopedia of Britain and Ireland gives an overview of any given period of British history. Just click on the text and you'll see a detailed outline of events.

CONTACT POINTS

Ordnance Survey Interactive Atlas of Great Britain
Price: £19.99*
Focus Multimedia
Tel: 01899 579 977
www.focusmm.co.uk

AA Where To Go in Britain and Ireland
Price: £19.99*
AA Interactive Encyclopedia of Britain and Ireland
Price: £19.99*
BTL
Tel: 01274 203 250
www.btlpublishing.com   *UK prices

Early learning – letters, sounds and words

Here we look at CD-ROMs that help children to recognize letters and words, laying a firm foundation for future learning.

Developing an early ability and understanding of basic reading and writing skills is increasingly important in today's crowded curriculum. Software companies have recognized this need and have combined the Multimedia capabilities of a PC with the visual effects popular with the very young to produce some excellent CD-ROMs that will give any child a head start with their ABCs.

● First words

It's a fact that today's children respond immediately to animated cartoon characters. It's therefore no wonder that so many CD-ROMs focusing on teaching literacy have cartoon hosts which lead children through all the games and reading challenges. Some even use the cartoon character's own story as the basis of the educational adventure.

This is the approach taken by Mindscape's *Reader Rabbit* series of early learning CD-ROMs. In *Reader Rabbit Nursery* (for ages three to five), for example, children use their pre-reading and problem-solving skills to return the sparkle to Reader Rabbit and Sam the Lion's home town of Sparkalot. In *Reader Rabbit Junior* (for ages four to six), the task is to help the cartoon heroes get back their Dreamship from Pointy Palace.

The *Reader Rabbit* series continues for older infants with titles labelled

*Mindscape's **Reader Rabbit** turns literacy into a travelling adventure, helping children of both nursery and junior school age get to grips with reading.*

Year 1 (ages five to seven) and *Year 2* (ages six to eight), each featuring new adventures and covering relevant aspects of the school curriculum. The activities, which include maths and science as well as reading, vocabulary and grammar, adjust themselves automatically to the child's skill level. Children can also choose to play in Adventure or Practice modes if they prefer.

● Fun with phonics

Learning to read and write for the first time is challenging, and is much more than just a matter of

recognising letter forms. In order to speak the words properly, a child must first master the familiar sounds of the language itself. *Phonic Spelling* from the *Full Marks* range of educational CD-ROMs tackles this problem for very young minds.

Phonic Spelling is split into twelve topics covering issues such as rhymes, same-ending words, silent letters and vowel sounds. Everything is taught using a fun gaming environment. You can print off graded certificates of achievement to provide additional encouragement for the child, and produce itemized reports for your own analysis, thereby enabling you to monitor progress and ensure that they attain the required targets for their age.

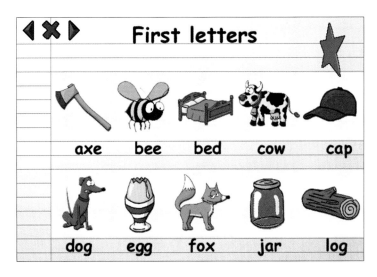

First letters

axe · bee · bed · cow · cap

dog · egg · fox · jar · log

Mary had a little lamb.

Its fleece was white as snow.

Full Marks Phonic Spelling begins with simple associations before tackling more challenging tasks such as missing vowels, rhyming words and silent letters. This title is designed to take children all the way from early reading right up to Key Stage 1.

DK Reading Made Easy features animated cartoon characters and games, while never losing sight of the fundamentals of reading. Here children can flick through an on-screen book of familiar rhymes and poems.

Play & Explore – Learn To Read takes a more conventional approach to helping preschoolers to pick up the fundamentals of the language. Aimed at three- to five-year-olds, this CD-ROM presents a progressive set of lessons comprising 60 games, puzzles, stories and activities to get children familiar with the alphabet and start reading before they leave playgroup. A nice touch is the library feature which stores all of the rhymes, songs and stories that are in the program so that children can listen to their favourites. There's even a mini word processor included.

● Developing vocabulary

Two products from the Dorling Kindersley stable have been designed to encourage the development of all aspects of early language skills. *Starting To Read* from the *My First CD-ROM* series uses games, songs, animation and print activities to introduce letter recognition and phonics as well as spelling patterns to the very young. Then *Reading Made Easy* takes children to Key Stage 1, supporting the literacy teaching in schools. Importantly, the interface is very different between the two programs: *Starting To Read* is hosted by White Bear and Penguin, while the cooler Kim and Dan characters guide you through *Reading Made Easy*.

Providing children with a head start in the English language is certain to pay off, and it won't cost an absolute fortune either.

Contents

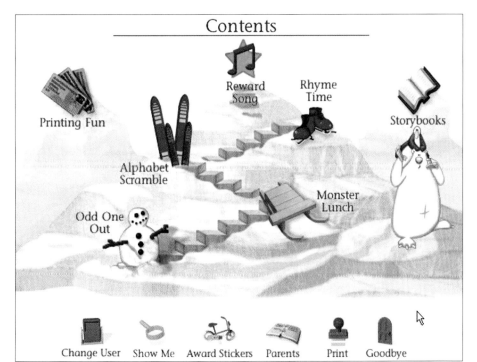

Printing Fun · Reward Song · Rhyme Time · Storybooks · Alphabet Scramble · Odd One Out · Monster Lunch · Change User · Show Me · Award Stickers · Parents · Print · Goodbye

In Dorling Kindersley's My First CD-ROM – Starting To Read, the emphasis is on making reading fun with activities to help build vocabulary skills. The main Contents menu uses 'picture' buttons to assist those still learning their letters.

CONTACT POINTS

Reader Rabbit series:
Nursery, Junior, Year 1, Year 2
Price: £20 each*
Mindscape
Tel: 01293 651300
www.mindscape.co.uk

Full Marks Phonic Spelling
Price: £9.99*
Idigicon
Tel: 01302 310800
www.idigicon.com

Play & Explore – Learn To Read
Price: £9.99*
Dorling Kindersley:
My First CD-ROM –
Starting To Read
Price: £9.99*
Dorling Kindersley:
Reading Made Easy
Price: £9.99*
GSP
Tel: 01480 460206
www.gsp.cc

*UK prices

Early learning programs

If you're a parent, you'll want your children to get an educational head start. Early learning programs help them – and you – to make the grade.

There's more pressure than ever on parents to get their children's education started before they begin school. The pressure continues too, as there's then the need for children to meet the requirements of the National Curriculum and the various Key Stages designed to measure a child's progress through the school system.

Fortunately, you can make use of your PC's Multimedia function to give your children a head start. There's plenty of early learning software available on CD-ROM software and it's a great way to make education fun.

● Introducing Hopsalot

Unlike TV programmes designed for preschoolers, you will find that the CD-ROMs aimed at the same age group are considerably more structured in terms of educational content. As well as helping children to learn, they introduce youngsters to the concept of school itself.

A good example of this kind of early learning title is Focus Multimedia's *Jump Ahead Starting School*, hosted by a cartoon rabbit named Hopsalot. Using an interactive classroom as the central point, children are encouraged to take part in 16 activities which combine play with education. They learn all the basics, from the alphabet and counting to rhyming, ordering, shapes and colours.

Jump Ahead Starting School's *Hopsalot the rabbit focuses on the classroom as the child's learning base rather than trying to teach by stealth. This interactive classroom leads to other rooms and playground sections where children can try out the many educational games on offer.*

Just as importantly, however, children are familiarised with the conventions of a classroom setup rather than that of a playgroup. So the CD-ROM provides a useful preparation for the move from playgroup to school.

Jump Ahead Starting School also has controllable features for parents. You can adjust the difficulty level to suit your child's age and ability, obtain some feedback from the program's built-in assessment technology, and print out workbooks as required.

● Games for toddlers

The *Play & Explore* series from GSP covers all of early learning, from the moment a child starts talking up until their final days at primary school. Two of the *Play & Explore* CD-ROMs are designed for the very first steps on the educational ladder: *Toddlers* and *Starting School*.

Toddlers is firmly aimed at children aged between two and four who may not even have experienced playgroup yet. There are eight games and activities to get involved in, from on-screen jigsaws to a xylophone music maker. The approach taken is to let children watch and listen, then gradually offer them entry points to take part themselves. In 'Who Are You?' for example, children are presented with an animated farmyard where they must listen to a sound and follow clues to discover which animal

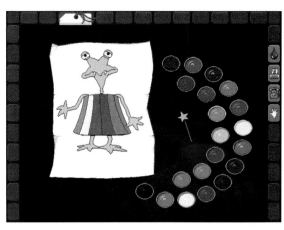

Play & Explore – Toddlers (left) seeks to stimulate rather than lecture. The artbox lets children paint masterpieces and create greetings cards.

In Play & Explore – Starting School (right) children learn more about colour by conjuring up their own monster to paint!

it belongs to. Or in 'Clever Colours' they can just mess around with paints on a digital canvas before moving on to more structured activities such as creating greetings cards.

The *Starting School* CD-ROM has a similar approach but takes three to five year olds nearer to those first days at real school in reception class. For example, in 'At The Zoo' you must colour the animals correctly and match the pairs. There are nine games and activities in total, each with multiple levels to maintain interest.

● **Dorling Kindersley**
The famous Dorling Kindersley brand has also produced a number of early learning CD-ROMs that sit alongside their well-known educational and reference titles for older children. Most notable is the *My First CD-ROM* series, which includes *Toddler School* and *Getting Ready for School*.

Toddler School is the kind of program you can run with your child sitting on your lap at first but, once they have the hang of using a mouse,

you'll be able to let them play on their own. It supports basic foundation skills such as recognising shapes and colours, responding to sounds and music, and putting things into order. There are six easy games to play, along with a collection of printable activities, all introduced by a friendly on-screen guide, a jack-in-the-box called Zak.

Zak returns in the follow-up CD-ROM, *Getting Ready for School*. Aimed at three to five year olds, this title tackles everyday issues such as number and letter recognition, logic, counting and alphabet sounds.

The disc includes resources for parents too, including an overview of child development and an outline of the educational aims of each section of the CD-ROM. You can adjust the

level of difficulty and game speeds to suit age and ability, while the software itself monitors your child's success rate and adjusts the amount of animated clues and help accordingly.

● **Triple packs**
Increasingly, early learning software is sold in pairs or as triple packs. The idea is to provide a one-stop purchase covering preschool reading, writing and numeracy. One such pack is *Top of the Class – Preschool*, which comprises three CD-ROMs (*Practise Reading*, *Practise Sums* and *Ted's Picnic Adventure*) in one box.

As well as offering value for money, these packs can provide a fast-track solution to getting your children prepared if they are due to start school soon.

Jump Ahead Starting School (above) begins with the very basics, using familiar equipment.

Getting Ready for School from Dorling Kindersley's My First CD-ROM series (left) is carefully designed for younger users who are about to enter reception year.

General knowledge on DVD

Massive multi-volume encyclopedias have been combined to make single-disc DVD-ROM products, which present a Multimedia-rich reference for homework, research or just to satisfy a hunger for knowledge.

Amerca was still a collection of British colonies when the first *Encyclopaedia Britannica* was published, back in 1768. Nearly 240 years later, it remains the world's best-known repository of facts and figures, and has grown into the heavyweight set of 32 bound books that everyone recognizes. Now, however, you can access all that information on a single DVD-ROM disc instead.

The sheer quantity of data has always presented a problem to serious computer-based encyclopedias as one CD-ROM simply isn't enough. But the capacious DVD-ROM format and the proliferation of DVD-ROM drives in home computers has now opened the way for a new approach. Putting an entire encyclopedia onto one DVD ends the frustration of disc-swapping and provides more space for Multimedia and other extras to enhance the learning experience.

● **Bring on the Brits**
Encyclopaedia Britannica 2003 Ultimate Reference Suite DVD crams all 32 print volumes onto just one disc. In addition, taking advantage of

the space on DVD-ROM, the title comprises three versions of the encyclopedia: the full library as you'd expect, a student version for school research, and an elementary version for 7 to 12 year olds.

Encyclopaedia Britannica lets you search by word and phrase, or more interactively by typing in the first few letters of a word and then scrolling through the potential matches it instantly brings up. Alternatively, you can choose to click on a single initial letter to browse the vast content alphabetically, just as you might with the print edition. Suggested matching entries appear in a list down the left hand side of the screen; clicking on any of them calls up that entry in its own window. *Encyclopaedia Britannica* entries are comprehensively cross-referenced so it's also easy to

The thematic Timeline view in Encyclopaedia Britannica displays key events in history along with click-through links to full articles and associated entries.

You may be surprised at the depth in which topics are covered in Encyclopaedia Britannica. Here, a simple search on the word 'snowboarding' calls up technical detail on snowboard equipment manufacture and sporting terrain, plus a demonstration video.

open up further windows for associated entries, images and articles.

The encyclopedia includes an atlas of 1,300 maps, each featuring clickable links on towns, cities and geographical areas to related text entries and pictures. There is also a thematic timeline for browsing topics over history. For example, you might decide to click on the Medicine theme and scroll along the timeline to locate significant events. Browsing in this way means that you could find out about the discovery of the rabies vaccine without knowing to search for Louis Pasteur first.

An innovative method of browsing through the *Encyclopaedia Britannica* is by using its unique, animated KnowledgeNavigator. This is a small window presenting a circle of topic titles; when you click on one, it moves to the centre and an array of related subtopics form a new circle around it. You can continue in

Maps in Encarta Premium Suite can be viewed in many styles from political and lingual to satellite images by day and night, while Map Treks give you further insight into the history of key regions.

Encarta Premium Suite offers plenty of Multimedia enhancements over traditional print encyclopedias, such as this 360-degree interactive panorama of the dome above Berlin's rebuilt Reichstag.

this manner to home in on the information you want or effectively 'surf' the topics to find less obviously associated entries.

● Modern favourite

Microsoft's best-selling encyclopedia *Encarta* began life on CD-ROM and has never existed in print. Now, the four-CD Premium Suite edition is also available as a single-disc DVD-ROM, complete with additional entries and Multimedia. You can still search by word and phrase as in *Encyclopaedia Britannica*, but *Encarta* encourages more relaxed use with its magazine-style approach.

Starting on the home screen, you can choose from a number of areas in which the encyclopedia's information has already been organised for you. For example, you can jump straight to the Statistics Centre for facts and figures, or the Multimedia Centre in order to access the videos and audio files in one place. There's even a Games Centre where you can test your knowledge of historic figures, events, visual landmarks and so on.

The Article Centre is the most useful area of the DVD-ROM for casual browsing, and these articles are well prepared with links to other places in the volume. *Encarta Premium Suite* also borrows from its World Atlas range of

CD-ROMs, presenting some of the most comprehensive maps – including satellite shots – you'll find anywhere. Its interactive virtual flights over the different continents are the kind of feature you couldn't possibly reproduce in a paper reference book.

Inevitably, *Encarta Premium Suite* also provides extensive links to related articles on the Internet, and registered users can download regular updates from the Web in order to keep the encyclopedia current.

● Instant reporting

Both *Encyclopaedia Britannica* and *Encarta Premium Suite* have added well-stocked software dictionaries to their DVDs, as well as some clever report-generating utilities. One of the most useful is the Researcher feature

obfuscate [ób fuss kayt, óbfəss kayt] (*3rd person present si...* obfuscates, *present participle* obfuscating, *past* obfuscated, *participle* obfuscated)
v

1. *vti* make something obscure: to make something obscur... especially by making it unnecessarily complicated
... to make something dark

Encarta's Dictionary gives quick definitions and thesaurus alternatives, while also providing instant translations between English, German, French, Spanish and Italian.

where every time you locate some information worth noting in the encyclopedias you can send it straight to the Researcher program.

This information could be text from an article, pictures, diagrams or even just some notes you have typed up while browsing. You can then run the Researcher utility to edit this mass of data and have it automatically re-organised into a logical project, which can be laid out as an attractive, printable report – great for school or college projects. Encarta's Researcher goes one step further by including a chart-generating program, so you can turn comparative statistics quickly into pie charts and histograms. Printed encyclopedias will always maintain their tactile appeal, but this new wave of single-disc DVD-ROM reference works can make research faster and more appealing for the PC owner. The pursuit of knowledge and the mundane preparation of school projects will never be the same again.

CONTACT POINTS

Encyclopaedia Britannica 2003 Ultimate Reference Suite DVD
Price: £59.99*
Encyclopaedia Britannica
Tel: 0800 282433
www.britannica.co.uk

Microsoft Encarta Premium Suite 2003 DVD
Price: £69.50*
Microsoft
Tel: 0870 601 0100
www.microsoft.com/uk/encarta

*UK prices

The Internet

Getting around faster

You've already learned how to use a browser to click on hot links and move around different Web pages. Now you can add some simple techniques to make it even quicker to visit your favourite sites.

Hyperlinks are the simplest way of surfing the World Wide Web (see Stage 1, page 135). Browsers also have built-in features, such as Back and Forward buttons, which make it even easier for you to navigate through linked web pages. If you use the browser's features in conjunction with hyperlinks, you will find you can move around the Web even more quickly and easily.

● Moving backwards and forwards
These buttons do just what they say. If you have visited several pages in one session, the Back button lets you step back to any of them without having to type in the page's address.

The Back button's 'history list' (see below) by default stores the last 20 Web pages that you have visited. If you want, you can adjust this setting via the Internet Options command in the Tools menu, to store more visited pages. Once you have used the Back button, the Forward button will take you to the next Web address on the list. Using these buttons together with hyperlinks (also called hot links) enables you to surf the Web quickly and efficiently.

● Go straight there
If you want to return to a site that is a number of pages back, you can use the menu that appears when you click on the small, downward-pointing arrow next to the Back button. This menu lists the last few Web pages you have visited. Clicking on any entry in this list will take you straight to that page. It's much quicker to use this list to jump several pages at a time than to click on the Back button repeatedly.

● Favourite places

The more you use the Internet, the more fascinating sites you will discover. It makes sense to return to your favourite places without hunting through search results and links every time you want to see them.

Some of the URLs for Internet sites are long and almost impossible to remember, but both Microsoft's Internet Explorer and Netscape's Navigator have thoughtfully made it easy to find your favourite sites time and time again by using what Explorer calls 'Favorites' and Netscape calls 'Bookmarks'.

These are easily accessed from a pull-down menu and then you just click on the name of the site you wish to re-visit to go straight there. Using Favorites and filing them sensibly will speed up your Internet use dramatically, as you will always be able to go straight to the pages you want to see and spend less and less time waiting for search engines to come back with results.

IF THE FAVORITE DOESN'T WORK

One of the most exciting things about the Internet is that it's constantly changing. This means that as sites grow in size and popularity, the person in charge of the site (known as the Webmaster) may have to move the location of all the information to an address that is capable of handling greater traffic and this can result in your Favorites not working. If you get an error message when you try to access a site, leave it for a few minutes and try again as it may have been busy. At other times, the site may be in the process of being updated and there will be a message telling you why it doesn't work and advising when to try accessing the site again. If the site has moved to a new address, you may be forwarded automatically or you'll have to click on a link to go there.

HTTP/1.0 404 Object Not Found

Bookmarks in Netscape Web browsers

Internet Explorer is not the only Web browser. One of the most popular alternatives is from Netscape. Many of its features – including bookmarks – are similar to the commands in Internet Explorer.

1 Browsing with Netscape Navigator, we have come across this mountain biking site. The address is www.mtbr.com and we think we'd like to visit it again although we don't want to have to remember or write down the address.

2 Click on the Bookmarks menu and a list of folders appears. These contain a selection of bookmark folders already provided by Netscape. Select Bookmark This Page to start compiling your own collection. Don't worry if you aren't sure if you want to revisit the site – bookmarks are easy to delete. When you are bookmarking, you are not subscribing to the site in any way, but simply making a note of its address for your browser.

3 Whichever Web page you are currently viewing is added to the Bookmarks menu. Take a look and you will see that it has been added at the bottom of the list of bookmarks. Notice that the site gives its bookmark the same name as the Web page's title. Each time you choose a bookmark in this way, it's added to the bottom of the list. You can add as many bookmarks as you like.

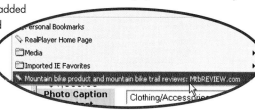

4 To organize your bookmarks, select Manage Bookmarks from the Bookmarks menu. This brings up a window that allows you to add folders, delete your old bookmarks and make other similar changes.

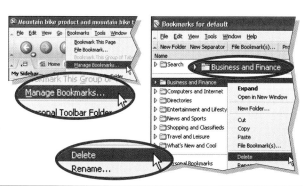

Add your favourite sites to Internet Explorer

Web addresses are easy to forget – especially long ones – so if you find a Web site that you want to visit again later, it's a good idea to add it to your Favorites list.

1 When you find a site you'd like to bookmark, click your way through its links until you get to the exact page you're interested in. It's better to make a bookmark for this page instead of the site's home page because it's usually quicker to download than the home page and saves you having to click your way through the site each time.

2 To bookmark a page in Internet Explorer, go to the Favorites drop-down menu at the top of the screen while you are looking at the page on the Web and click on Add to Favorites.

3 A new window appears offering a variety of options. As well as simply adding the site to your Favorites, you can change its name, and make it available to view when you are not connected to the Internet by checking the Make available offline box. You can also select an existing folder to put it in, or create a new folder. For now, just click on OK to add it to your Favorites list with its existing name.

4 The Favorite is added instantly. When you next start Internet Explorer, one click on the page's name in the Favorites menu will take you back to that Web page immediately.

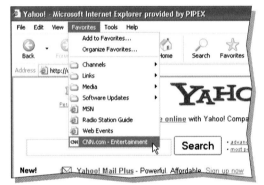

REARRANGING FAVORITES

You can move Favorites by dragging them with the mouse. Click on the Favorites menu and position the mouse over the Favorite you want to move. Now click and, while holding down the left mouse button, drag the Favorite to a folder. The folder automatically opens, allowing you to drop the Favorite into the new position.

5 To remove Favorites you no longer want, just click on Organize Favorites in the Favorites menu and a new window appears. Highlight the Favorite you want to remove and then click on the Delete button. The Favorite is instantly removed.

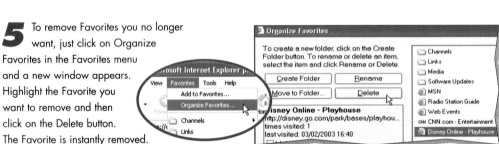

6 Using folders helps to keep the Favorites menu organized. To create a folder, click on the Create Folder button in the Organize Favorites dialog box and then give the new folder a name.

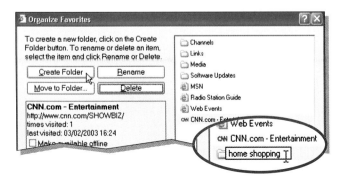

7 You can save new Favorites into these new folders. Once the Web page has loaded, select Add to Favorites from the Favorites menu. However, before clicking on the OK button in the Add Favorite dialog box, select a folder from the Create in list. You can also move Favorites between folders (see Rearranging Favorites box, above).

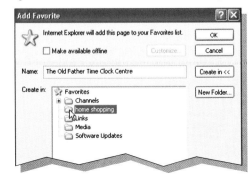

Faster Favorites and older History

When you want to retrace your Internet steps, Internet Explorer has two useful panels that can save lots of clicking through menus and help out if your memory draws a blank.

1 Within a few weeks of surfing and saving Favorites, it's likely that the Favorites menu will have grown considerably. Adding folders to organize Favorites into categories of Web sites is therefore a great idea.

2 However, the more folders you add, and the more categories you create in your Favorites menu, the more clicking around the Favorites menu you have to do when you want to revisit a site. This Favorite, for example, is three levels deep.

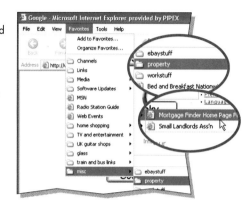

3 The quick way to navigate through lots of folders and files is to switch on the Favorites panel. Click once on the Favorites button on the toolbar and a panel opens on the left of the Internet Explorer window.

4 Click on this list of Favorites – unlike the Favorites menu, the folders don't disappear from view each time you use them, so this is a much quicker way to surf to your favourite sites.

5 Of course, there will always be times when you've simply forgotten to bookmark a site, the address of which you can't remember. However, if you know that you visited the site quite recently, use the History panel. Just click once on the toolbar's History button.

6 The Favorites panel will disappear, to be replaced by a History panel. This lists all the sites you have visited recently. The current Web page – which, in this example, is Google – is now highlighted in the History list.

PC TIPS

Choosing an order

Although it is usually most useful to view sites in the History Panel in date order, Internet Explorer can sort the list by other criteria to help you find the site you're looking for. Click on the View button at the top of the History panel and select an option from the drop-down menu that appears.

7 Scroll back up to the top of the History panel and you'll see that Internet Explorer has arranged the Web sites according to the date you visited them. This means that if you know you visited a particular site last week, just click on the Last Week entry.

8 The Last Week entry expands to show all the sites you visited. Browse the list and click on any site that seems familiar. A list of the pages you visited on the site appears – click on one to revisit the page.

Help with your site

It's easy to create your own Web site but, to make a site effective, interesting and easy to navigate, you might benefit from some of the help that is freely available on the Web.

With the Internet's growing popularity, more and more people are deciding that they want to build their own Web site. We introduced you to Hyper Text Mark-up Language (HTML) in Stage 3, pages 132–135, where we showed you that creating a personal Web site is within reach of even the most inexperienced user.

However, this can be something of a double-edged sword, for although it might be easy enough to produce a fairly simple Web page, it's a rather more demanding task to create one that looks good, is easy to use and works flawlessly. It can often be difficult to find reliable, concrete help about site design but the Internet is a great source of design information – if you know where to find it. Over the next few pages we'll be looking at sites that, in their various ways, will help you to make a better site.

● Technical issues

The most obvious way a Web site can help you is by providing detailed explanations of technical terms and issues. There are many sites devoted to teaching HTML, most of which include information resources, **FAQs** and noticeboards. Descriptions, in varying degrees of detail, of all the current HTML commands and functions are common and can be very useful when you have a specific query or project in mind.

Sites often feature programming tutorials and examples of popular items, such as tables and forms. Other useful sites help out in different ways by automating particular aspects of Web design, perhaps by creating a logo for you, mixing a colour palette or giving your Web site a free chat room; you'll soon find that there is much more to HTML help resources than mere explanations of jargon.

Pretty quickly, however, you will discover that technical issues are not the only problems in making your Web site; it can be very difficult for someone without an art or design background to create a readable and user-friendly site. This aspect of Web site creation is often ignored, but you should not under-estimate its importance. After all, if your site is incomprehensible, or its layout illogical, no amount of tricks will make people linger to figure out where to find the interesting material.

For every stage of Internet site creation there is help available over the Internet.

Finding help on the Internet

For every stage of creating successful Internet pages there is somewhere to go for advice. Here we look at some popular and useful Web sites that will help you to get your work noticed.

CREATING YOUR own Internet site can be both exciting and daunting. Deciding what information to include is the enjoyable part, whether it is a site dedicated to your personal interests or hobbies, or just to announce your existence to the world. It is the technical aspects that are more complicated. From HTML code and page design to ways of ensuring that people browsing the Internet will come across your site, we show you where to find help.

WebReference.com

www.webreference.com

Keeping up with anything to do with the Internet can be tricky. With the whole world contributing to its content, and technology advancing as fast as it is, it can be very difficult to keep abreast of all the latest breakthroughs and developments. This is particularly true with HTML as new versions, tools and extras are appearing all the time. To help you maintain your knowledge you might want to keep an eye on this site.

It's called WebReference and, while it contains plenty of technical references and tutorials, many visitors find it extremely useful for its up-to-date information.

There are some particularly interesting sections dealing with topics not always covered by more elementary sites, such as XML and 3D animation. Useful lessons and articles from experts on topics such as 3D, graphics, HTML and JavaScript are all archived for future reference. In short, if you want to find up-to-date information on all areas of Web design, WebReference is the site to visit.

WDG: Web Design Group

www.htmlhelp.com

The Web Design Group Web site is one of the most respected and authoritative resources for HTML information on the Web, covering the entire spectrum of HTML variations and uses. The Web Authoring Reference section is particularly useful and complete. This features a large

area on the latest version of HTML, describing all the possible uses and syntax. It also goes into extra detail on other complex issues, such as cascading style sheets and character sets. You'll also find a series of FAQs, a guide to design considerations, downloadable tools, links to other relevant sites and feature articles.

Web Style Guide

www.webstyleguide.com

The importance of a well-designed Web site has become even more apparent in recent years. Little thought was previously given to whether individual features on a site actually worked well – the fact that they could be achieved was sufficient. This has led to some of the problems that any Web surfer will be familiar with: sites that take a long time to load; technically impressive sites that don't contain any of the information you are looking for; and poorly designed sites that don't deliver on their over-ambitious promises.

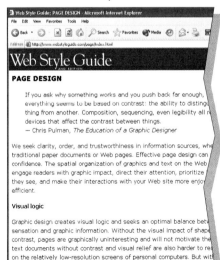

This is an excellent site for those who want to ensure that their site is as practical as possible. In keeping with its no-nonsense remit, this site lacks unnecessary frills. Don't be put off by the uninspiring design – it's full of great advice on making your site as user-friendly as possible.

Web Pages That Suck

www.webpagesthatsuck.com

This famous site uses badly designed sites to help visitors to distinguish between good and bad Web design. It gives examples of what not to do and then attempts to describe where a design has gone wrong, so that you know what to avoid when you are creating your own site. Most of the pages selected are business or entertainment sites, so you don't have to feel bad about laughing at some unfortunate first-timer's early HTML experiments. Take the tour of the various sites: each illustrates a particular design flaw and has plenty of good – and entertaining – suggestions on how to avoid it.

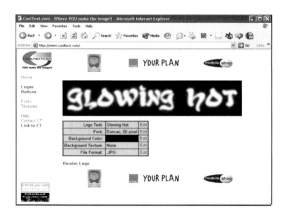

CoolText.com

www.cooltext.com

CoolText is a handy site that creates logos and styles text for your Web pages. You create your text by typing in the words you wish to use and then select from various font styles, sizes and depths. These selections are made by clicking on a number of example graphics and editing your choices. When you're satisfied with your selections, you can tell CoolText to render your logo so that you can take a look at it. If you're happy with it, you can download the logo and add it to your own site.

Newark1 Web Design Guide

www.newark1.com/color

The Newark1 Web Design Guide helps with one aspect of designing your site that should really be easy, but usually isn't: choosing colours for your text, backgrounds and graphics. This site offers some sound advice on the appropriate colours to use according to the message that your Web site is trying to put across, and explains how colours complement and interact with each other. It also provides examples of Web pages and comments on how the colours used work together.

Doctor HTML

www2.imagiware.com/RxHTML

Nobody likes proof-reading their own work, and it's even less fun checking dozens of Web site links or wading through mountains of HTML code. Doctor HTML is essential for those who don't relish this task, or are too busy to do it themselves.

You can set Doctor HTML to automatically search through either a single page or an entire site, checking for spelling mistakes, syntax errors, bad links and missing pictures. It then provides a summary of its findings in a report.

Web Marketing Info Center

www.wilsonweb.com/webmarket

Although a significant number of personal Web sites are created simply for the amusement of the author, many people use them to help their business or to run their own Internet sideline. In this case, design and content becomes rather more important. After all, if your site is just a shrine to your favourite pop star, it doesn't really matter if it's badly designed, but if it is intended as a means of augmenting your income, you need to make sure it's slick and user friendly.

This site contains articles on how to organize a business site. These include all the vital design and organization questions – What is your site for? Who are you hoping to attract? How is it advertised? Does it look pleasing to the eye? Suggestions and pointers are offered, as is advice about where to go for further reading and help.

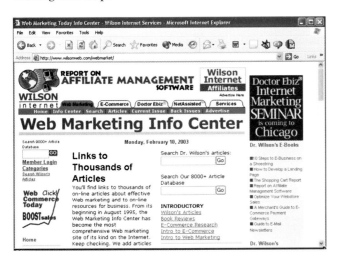

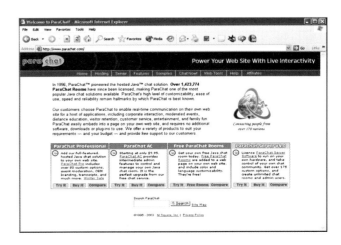

ParaChat

www.parachat.com

If you've ever visited a Web site and wondered how they implement such apparently advanced features as chat rooms or guest books for visitors, console yourself with the thought that the Web designer probably didn't have anything to do with it. Nowadays, anyone can host their own chat room simply by filling in an application form. The basic versions of the Parachat series of chat rooms are completely free to almost anyone. The ParaChat Group makes its money by running little banner adverts alongside the chat area, allowing you to have a fully featured room all to yourself. Visit this site to apply for your own room; if you are accepted, you can define the subject matter of the room and specify the design of the chat area of your Web site. All you then need to do to get the room up and running is to copy a couple of lines of HTML code supplied by the ParaChat site to the top of your chat page.

Add Me!

www.addme.com

You've finished your Web site, added a chat room, checked the links, created an attractive logo and uploaded everything to the Internet. The only problem is that you've had only three visitors in the past week and you suspect that at least two of them were yourself! The final problem you'll encounter when creating a Web site is getting your work noticed; unless your Web site is properly advertised, nobody is going to know it's there. The mysterious workings of search engines, such as Yahoo and Lycos, mean that many Web sites – even some of the very best ones – fail at this final hurdle. As a result, a whole service industry has evolved offering help in promoting your site.

Many sites charge for their work but a number, such as Add Me!, are more charitable and offer free help and advice on getting noticed. This largely comes down to registering your URL with as many search engines as possible – the top 14 in the case of Add Me! – adding special HTML to describe your site's contents accurately,

and ensuring that you have an appropriate 'title' for each page of your site. If you check out this site and use the advice it offers, you should reduce the risk of Web surfers missing out your Web site when they use search engines to travel around the Net.

Dealing with junk email

There's no shortage of sources of irritation on the Internet, but such annoyances are nothing compared to the rage Internet users reserve for the cyberspace equivalent of junk email, commonly known as 'spam'.

The hatred with which many Internet users regard spam cannot be underestimated. This might seem strange at first, especially as an email message can be destroyed or deleted far more quickly and surely than any physical junk mail. But unlike physical junk mail, spam costs you time and money. It's you who is paying to download it – and you won't even know what it is until you do.

Another irritating factor is the subject matter that most spam contains. You might think getting real junk mail about credit cards you already own is annoying, but most spam seems to be a thinly disguised chain letter, a pyramid scheme, or worse still, an invitation to visit a Web site containing adult material from which any children using the Web need to be protected.

● Random mailing

In addition, the fact that spam is usually completely random in its targets also serves to annoy. Needless to say, the vast majority of spam mail emanates from the United States. Getting your 100th invitation to pay an extortionate fee and join an over-80s golf club in Miami can become very tiresome – particularly if you're a 25-year-old in Australia.

Spam isn't just limited to email messages. Similar messages that are posted on newsgroups are also referred to as spam, for precisely the

Although the word 'spam' refers to a particular brand of luncheon meat, when used in conjunction with the Web it is a very disparaging term for unwanted email.

same reason. The close-knit nature of many newsgroups means that their regular visitors are especially incensed by spam, and often conduct extended witch hunts against any company or individual foolish enough to post an unsolicited advert on a newsgroup.

There is quite a degree of justification for this attitude, as many popular newsgroups have been ruined by an over abundance of spam, to the extent that all serious users eventually leave in disgust.

Spam is exceedingly difficult to prevent. After all, the Internet is still almost entirely unregulated, which means anyone can do pretty much

WHY IS INTERNET JUNK CALLED 'SPAM'?

The most widely accepted theory as to the origin of the word 'spam' is that it is a reference to a Monty Python song which went something along the lines of 'Spam, spam, spam, spam, spam, spam, spam, spam, spam, spam, spam, spam, spam, spam', and so on. The connection was that Internet spam is also a pointless repetition of meaningless words or information.

anything they like, at least in theory. Many people are of the opinion that democracy and free speech should not extend to annoying junk mail. As a result, many of the larger Internet service providers (ISPs) have instituted policies to prevent the so-called 'spammers' from sending out unsolicited emails, both by trying to stop known 'spammers' using their services altogether and by helping customers to block spam before they receive it. These policies are only partially successful, however, as spammers become ever more skilled at hiding the true content of an email from anyone, even including the recipient (see page 141).

● Minimizing spam
Despite this, there *are* some steps which the ordinary Web user can take to diminish their own personal tide of junk email. The two main methods are software solutions, and anti-spam lists and Web sites. Neither is 100 per cent successful, but using the two together can radically reduce the amount of junk email you receive.

Over the next few pages we look at some of the Web sites that can help you achieve a cyberspace heaven devoid of sales flyers.

Anti-spam sites
Try the methods these Internet sites offer to reduce the amount of unwanted spam email polluting your computer world.

CAUCE (Coalition Against Unsolicited Commercial Email)
www.cauce.org
This is the most high-profile and well-organized anti-spam group on the Web. It is a non-profit organization made up largely of technology workers, journalists and commentators who are fed up with receiving unwanted emails. CAUCE's Web site is professionally put together but is, like most anti-spam sites, mostly text-only. However, the site is packed with information on spam, and the pros and cons of different ways of dealing with it.

The main thrust of the group's efforts is to introduce anti-spam legislation via the US Congress. To help achieve this, US visitors are invited to write to their member of Congress and also to help promote the cause of CAUCE.

Spam-weary European citizens can also help raise CAUCE's profile by registering on the EuroCAUCE site (www.euro.cauce.org) and there are also sites for Australia (www.caube.org.au), Canada (http://cauce.ca) and India (www.india.cauce.org). At the EuroCAUCE site you can see figures that show just how big a problem spam is, and how direct marketing organizations are trying to fight anti-spam legislation. The site also keeps a record of how this legislation is progressing through the European courts.

Junkbusters
www.junkbusters.com
If you want to be more pro-active in the way you deal with spam, there are a number of actions you can take. The most common step usually involves giving your email details to an anti-spam list. This list then registers your address as one that does not want to receive any kind of unsolicited commercial email and forwards your details to any company that will listen.

This Web site offers to add you to a number of anti-spam lists, and can also add your postal address to a separate list so that you receive less 'real' junk mail and telephone marketing. The Junkbusters site also gives you a number of simple but helpful tips on how to avoid spam in general.

Network Abuse Clearinghouse

www.abuse.net/

If you have managed to find out the origin of the spam you've been receiving, then you should report your findings to the Network Abuse Clearinghouse.

There are many sites such as this where you can report spamming companies and Web domains, but this is one of the most level-headed and also provides advice and resources to help you fight known spammers. The Network Abuse Clearinghouse has a range of resources available. These include abuse reporting tools, which can help to determine where a message originated from and generate a complaint; intrusion detection and prevention resources; and even reviews on useful literature.

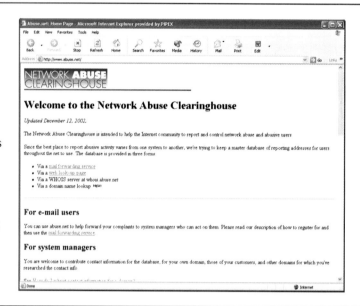

SPAM.Anti!

www.spamanti.net

Although they can usually produce very good results, anti-spam lists and software are only ever reactive in their approach to dealing with spam. The simple fact is that these 'spamming' companies are not just pulling email addresses out of the blue: they are receiving them from *somewhere*. If you can find a way to stop this flow of data, you can remove any chance of getting spam.

This site contains information about anti-spam lists, software and legal action, but it also includes a very helpful, online tutorial detailing how you can avoid getting spam in the first place. The central concept to avoiding spam is to be as anonymous as possible on the Internet and *not* to give your address out freely.

SpamKiller

www.mcafee.com

The heavyweight amongst anti-spam software is SpamKiller. Originally written by an independent Norwegian company, this award-winning program has now been bought by software giant McAfee. Its anti-spam function uses five different filters when examining incoming email. Not only does it look at the sender's address, it also checks the message text, the header, the country code and the subject field, and a Filter Wizard allows you to add your own filters. It also ensures that important emails do get through. SpamKiller makes a copy of all automatically filtered mail for uploading to the main SpamKiller site, where the information from the email can be added to the anti-spam database.

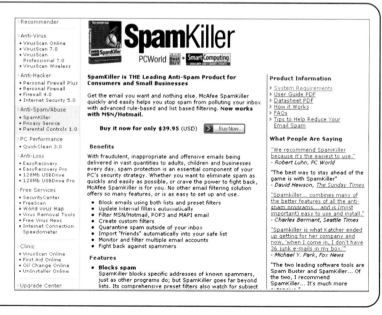

Junk email tricks

Spammers use many tricks to maximize the money they make from their mass emailings, and they may try to fool you to get a response.

WHILE A few direct marketing companies openly lobby governments to allow their spam, many Internet businesses have far fewer scruples. They use every trick in the book to increase profits – one popular ruse is to hide their real identities to avoid censure and complaint.

When you receive junk email it's tempting to reply and let them know how you feel, but that's almost never the right thing to do. In many cases it simply increases the amount of spam you'll receive in the future. Here are some examples of ploys used by spammers.

Unsubscribe links

You may receive spurious emails claiming that you have opted in to mailshots. These spammers hope that the message at the top of the email will persuade you to use the Unsubscribe link before pressing the [Delete] key. However, using these links will rarely produce the desired result (see Fresh email addresses box, below).

Faking a subject line

Spammers often use lies in an email's subject line to make you open their messages. In this case, 'Tom' seems to be asking for help, but the message is typical junk email. If you complain or attempt to unsubscribe, the spammers will be delighted to hear from you.

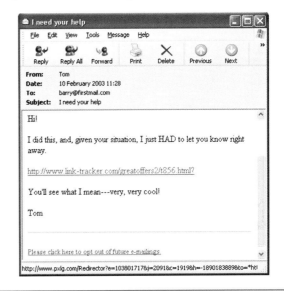

Showing an IP address

All Web sites have a four-part numerical code called an IP address although you rarely see them because they are difficult to understand. Some spammers hide their Web address in the links in their message, showing their IP address instead. They do this because they know that few people will be able to work out where the message came from.

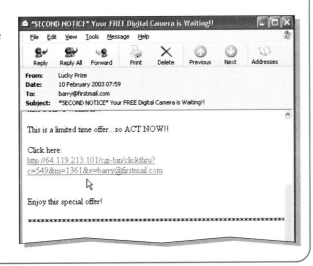

Internet banking

Using online banks has become a popular and widespread form of money management. Here we show you how easy it is to start banking on the Internet.

Telephone banking was a revolution of the 1980s; one free phone call at any time of day or night and you could pay bills, check balances, transfer funds, set up direct debits and all the rest. But that was yesterday's revolution.

Now, just about every bank you've ever heard of offers Internet banking. The beauty of using the Net is, of course, its ease of access and flexibility. With an Internet account you can do your banking from any PC connection, as you are logging on to the bank's site in cyberspace, rather than their physical offices. You can stay in control 24 hours a day from anywhere in the world, which is ideal if you travel for work or are on holiday.

● What you get
Most Internet banks offer a very similar range of services. Once you've logged in to your account (see Banking security box, right) you can check all your accounts – current, savings, ISAs, mortgages, and so on. You can also transfer money between them with just a few clicks. You can set up or amend direct debits and standing orders, and pay bills. All your current and historical data is there to be examined, and is easily downloaded to a spreadsheet or financial package, such as Quicken or Microsoft Money.

If you shop around and are prepared to change accounts, you can find some very attractive rates of interest on current and savings accounts,

Internet banking provides a quick and easy method of accessing and controlling your financial accounts, without having to make a trip to your high street bank.

substantially higher than those offered by standard bank accounts. These offers tend to be made by banks that are Internet-only operations, such as Smile, Egg and Cahoot. Do watch out though as these very attractive interest rates might not last for ever; while they reflect the banks' lower overheads, they are also 'loss leaders' to tempt a large number of new customers to sign on quickly.

● What you need
All you need for Internet banking are a PC, a modem and an ISP, although you may have to upgrade some software on your PC before you can start banking online. Check which browser and which version of it the service supports – many banks support both Internet Explorer and Netscape Navigator, but some require you to use Internet Explorer.

Once you sign up to Net banking, you will find the higher interest rates and the control over your finances that it provides are well worth it.

BANKING SECURITY

Is your money safe with an Internet bank? The answer is that it is going to be as safe as anything can be on the Internet. Nobody takes security more seriously than banks. All the services mentioned here use the highest levels of data encryption. In addition, there are thorough identity checks when you log on. Typically, you will have to enter your name and postcode, the password you have chosen, and an additional piece of information – such as your mother's maiden name, for example. All in all, it's pretty secure. But don't forget to take precautions at your end: if you save pages of data and leave them on your PC, you have only yourself to blame if the information is accessed by unauthorized viewers.

Using Internet banking

Here we use Nationwide (www.nationwide. co.uk) to show how easy it is to carry out banking tasks on the Web.

NATIONWIDE WAS one of the first building societies to set up Internet banking, and its Web site does a good job of explaining the services available. As you'd expect from a leading building society, there are also mortgages and

loans on offer. In addition, Nationwide makes its much-reported House Price Index accessible online, so you can get an idea of how house prices have changed in an area by typing in a postcode.

1 Use your Web browser to visit the www.nationwide.co.uk site. When the home page appears, click on the demo link in the Internet banking section and then click on the large link at the top of the next page.

2 The first screen illustrates the security checks, which require the account holder to enter three pieces of information specified when the account was set up. For this demo, the information is supplied for you, so just click on the Sign On Now button.

3 The Nationwide demonstration has four accounts already set up, covering Banking, Credit Card, Savings and Mortgage. Click on the account under the Banking heading.

4 This opens a page that shows an up-to-date statement for this current account. You can see the flow of money into and out of the account. There are also links to common tasks on the left of the screen. Click on the Payments & Transfers link.

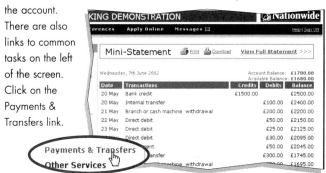

5 You would use this screen to pay bills and create standing orders. You can also use it to transfer money between accounts. Since this current account has a healthy balance, we can transfer some to our savings account. Click on the Transfer Money link at the top of the screen.

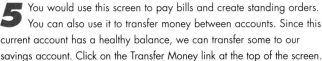

6 In the Transfer Money screen you can select the accounts you want to use in your transfer. The Available Balance box is automatically updated to show the maximum amount you can transfer. Type in an amount and click on the Transfer button.

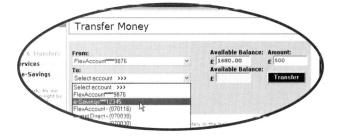

7 You'll be asked to confirm the transfer in a pop-up dialog box. Click on the OK button to continue. That's all there is to online banking – it's far easier than queueing and form-filling at the bank.

Accessing Internet banks

Here we review a few of the most prominent Internet bank sites on the Web.

NatWest

www.natwest.com

NatWest's online service allows you to run up to 50 accounts (current, deposit, credit card, and so on). The site provides a demonstration of their online services, which shows how to transfer money between accounts, set up and manage direct debits and standing orders, and carry out other common transactions. The site uses some security measures. For example, access to your account is protected by both PIN and password and, as soon as you log on, the date and time of your last session is shown so you can see if your accounts have been accessed by someone else. The NatWest online bank is compatible with both Internet Explorer and Netscape Navigator Web browsers.

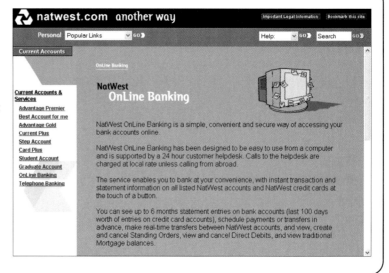

Smile

www.smile.co.uk

Smile is an Internet bank that was formed in 1999 by the Co-Operative Bank, and has been winning awards for customer-friendly design and security ever since. Like its parent, it follows ethical investment and customer service policies that are based on the original principles of the Co-Operative movement. You can use LINK cash machines for withdrawals and any Post Office for paying in both cash and cheques.

There's a simple slide-show that demonstrates how online banking works and you can start the process of switching from your existing bank using Smile's online forms. Smile has also diversified, adding mortgages, loans and credit cards to its online current account offering.

Cahoot

www.cahoot.com

The Internet-only division of Abbey National, Cahoot has lower overheads and is therefore able to offer more attractive interest rates on current accounts than its high-street parent. Because it's a new system and highly automated, it is also able to offer some features that are unavailable through traditional banks. For example, you can set up an automated alert that will send you an email or a text message on your mobile phone if your account falls below a certain level. Cahoot is working hard at adding new ways to access its accounts. On PCs, the system works with both Internet Explorer and Netscape Navigator web browsers, and it's also available via WAP mobile phones. There's a plan to make its accounts accessible via digital TV handsets too.

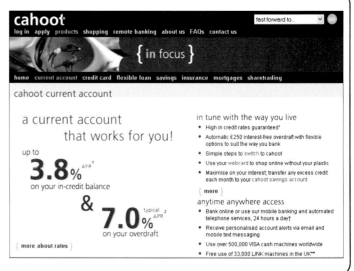

The Royal Bank of Scotland

www.rbs.co.uk

Compared to the bright and colourful design of many of the new Internet-only banks, the Royal Bank of Scotland's Web site is a far more restrained affair, and you'll need to look for the links to its Digital Banking section. Once there, you'll find links that can automatically test your PC and Web browser to see if they are suitable to use with the service.

You can also choose between two demonstrations: one is fully interactive – where you enter information such as the amount of money to transfer or the accounts to use – while the other demo takes a slide-show approach and adds more explanation. Unlike some Internet banks, however, you can't apply online – instead you need to fill in an on-screen form, print it out and send it by post.

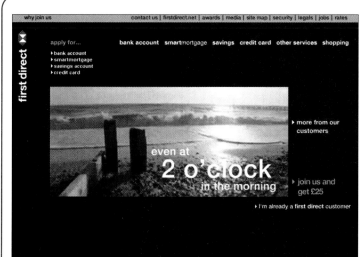

First Direct

www.firstdirect.com

The original telephone bank was, oddly, a little late in joining the Internet banking race but is now well established. First Direct offers a very similar type of online service to all the other Internet banking operations. Points to note, however, are that you cannot access the service from a PC connected to a local network (making it tricky to check your account from the office) and, although the First Direct system requirements don't specifically rule out Netscape Navigator, there's a strong recommendation that you use Internet Explorer.

Barclays

https://ibank.barclays.co.uk

Barclays was one of the first major banks to embrace the Internet with enthusiasm and you can see the benefits of that early investment in its Web site. The Internet banking option offers everything you'd expect, with the full range of accounts. It also shows you how it all works with a good demonstration.

The site offers links to Barclays' online stock dealing service, travel services and mortgages and loans. Like many online banks, Barclays understands that some potential customers are nervous of losing money through fraud on the Web. It therefore offers a guarantee to reimburse you for all losses if your account is used fraudulently.

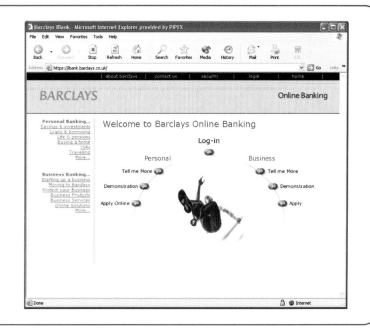

The great outdoors

When you're surfing the Web you can walk just about anywhere in the world that's worth a stroll, and all without leaving your PC screen.

Going out for a walk must be one of the most popular leisure pursuits in Britain, and quite possibly in the rest of the world as well. There is, after all, nothing quite like a breath of fresh air and a good view.

There are Web sites covering almost every aspect of outdoor activities. In this article, we'll limit ourselves to walking and its offshoots – some of which can be very strenuous and exotic pursuits.

● Country walks

Walking covers many different grades of activity. For some people it means getting in the car, driving to a beauty spot and then having a gentle stroll with, perhaps, a picnic or a pub lunch. This, however, is not the kind of walking that arouses great passion or obsession and, as a result, there are relatively few Web sites concentrating on this type of walking.

However, one outstanding site on this subject, the Conservation Walks site (countrywalks.defra.gov.uk), presented by the Department for Environment, Food and Rural Affairs, offers more than a thousand such walks in England. Unless you live in a very remote area, you'll be able to find a good selection of walks within easy driving distance.

● Hiking

A notch up from mere walking brings us into the realm of hiking which is regarded as a much more serious pursuit. Hiking is strenuous, needs planning, takes you to out-of-the-way places and often requires a certain

amount of specialist kit. As a result, hikers tend to be very enthusiastic about this activity. That's great news for the Web surfing enthusiast, because passion breeds Web sites; and there are certainly plenty of very good and informative sites that deal with hiking in the wilderness.

● Authoritative sites

Not all Web sites devoted to hiking are the exclusive province of walking fanatics though. There are plenty of authoritative sites from organizations that promote the interests of hikers and other outdoors people, for

The Web allows you to visit the highest peaks and see the most spectacular views – and ensures that you are properly dressed for all occasions.

example, the well-known Ramblers Association (www.ramblers.org.uk). The sites we feature here, such as the British Orienteering Federation and the Scottish Mountaineering Club, are also exemplary in their information and presentation.

● Enthusiasts' sites

It's the enthusiasts' sites that bring hiking to life. Those who have walked from Land's End to John O'Groats or

have spent weeks alone in the outback are all keen to share their tales. You'll find inspiring accounts of trips to just about every place on earth together with masses of practical advice and tips in these sites. Tourist and regional organizations also supply some good sites, but they tend to lack the tang of the enthusiast.

● **Getting the kit**

Anyone who spends a lot of time exploring the outdoors acquires a strong interest in the correct clothing and equipment – the rain-proof breathable jackets, three-season sleeping bags, state-of-the-art compass and so on. The Web is a great place for discovering what's new and what users think about it, as well as giving access to outlets around the nation and the ability to check and compare prices. Many outdoor sites have a 'gear' section, but for advice and an authoritative evaluation, the best guide is the Gear Guy, see page 148.

Start walking

Here's a good cross-section of outdoors sites, ranging from the individual and homespun to the commercial and slick.

Great Outdoor Recreation Pages (GORP)

www.gorp.com

This smart, magazine-style site covers not just walking and hiking, but also other outdoor pursuits, from tracking gorillas in the Congo to snowboarding in Europe. There's a featured area in every issue and good contributions from walkers as well as forums, indexed geographically, to allow visitors to swap notes with others.

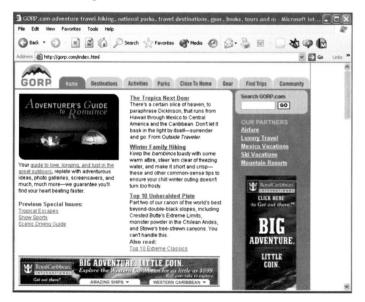

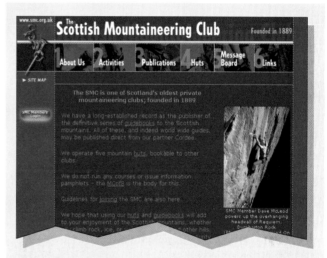

The Scottish Mountaineering Club

www.smc.org.uk

This pre-eminent organization guards the interests of climbers and, to a slightly lesser extent, walkers, in the Scottish Highlands. There is a section on hillwalking, mountains, huts and the 'Munros' – 284 Scottish peaks over 3,000ft high – first compiled by the Victorian walker Sir Hector Munro. It has become something of an obsession for many walkers to climb all the Munros. Once achieved, you can add your name to the list of 'compleatists'.

How to use a compass

www.uio.no/~kjetikj/compass

It's amazing how many people will go for a walk or hike in a remote part of the country, armed with a compass that they don't know how to use. If that includes you, then you should navigate immediately to Norwegian orienteer Kjetil Kjernsmos's illustrated guide on just how to find your way around with the compass. It's divided into a number of clearly illustrated and well-explained, step-by-step lessons.

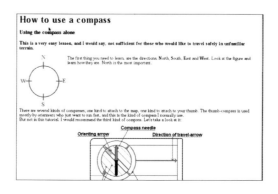

The Gear Guy

http://web.outsideonline.com/gear/gearguy

Douglas Gantenbein is the 'gear guy' in question, and his site is a mine of information. It's so well-respected that it has earned a substantial sub-section on the Outside site (www.outsidemag.com). The Gear Guy section works in a simple, interactive way: you send Doug a question, and he answers it, providing you with detailed and authoritative advice. Over time, a large archive of Q&As has built up, so you can probably find the advice you're after without even asking. If you need some size 21 boots, Doug can suggest someone who'll make them for you. Doug's answers relate only to US suppliers and their equipment but, as most of these have international distribution, he's still worth consulting.

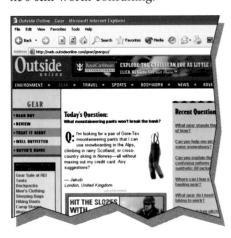

Trekking holidays

Plan the perfect walking holiday using the Web.

Explore Worldwide

www.exploreworldwide.com

This site features a wide range of tours and adventures, and also provides you with a reasonable amount of information. Sections from the company's brochure are supplied as individual PDFs, which you can download to get more detailed information on individual tours.

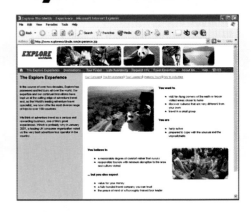

Trek Nepal

www.treknepal.co.uk

You'll find lots of solid detail about trekking holidays in Nepal in this enthusiast's personal Web site. A handy section on 'Life on the Trek' gives you an idea of what a trek might entail.

Exodus Travel

www.exodus.co.uk

This is the classiest of the three sites featured here, with very snazzy graphics, including slide shows. There are also excellent, detailed descriptions of the various treks available through Exodus Travel.

British Orienteering Federation

www.cix.co.uk/~bof

If you find that walking and hiking are not challenging enough for you, it could be time to try orienteering. This sport is Nordic in origin and involves running (or walking, depending on how you feel) through forests and up hills, passing by various checkpoints along the way. Map and compass skills are crucial, and a reasonable level of fitness is helpful although you do move at your own pace. For the newcomer, the BOF site answers all your questions about orienteering and what it entails. It also supplies a comprehensive list of fixtures and events, together with links to the large number of local clubs in Britain. For those already involved in orienteering, there are also news stories, results and rankings.

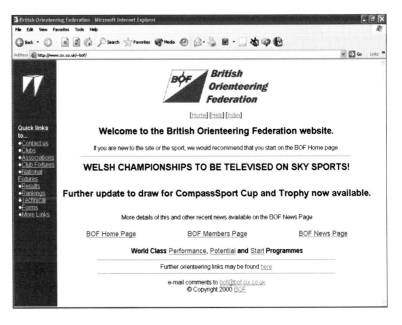

Cotswold Outdoor

www.cotswold-outdoor.com

One of the leading outdoor retailers in the UK, this is one of the better outdoor gear shops on the Web. It seems to stock pretty much all the leading brands in outdoor fashion and equipment. Most goods are clearly illustrated and are accompanied by sound technical information and, if you don't really know what you're looking for in a product, the site's technical guides will give helpful advice. There's also a 12-month guarantee and returns policy on any items you purchase.

Mountain Bothies Association

www.mountainbothies.org.uk

These are the people you should thank next time you shelter from an overnight storm in a remote Scottish mountain hut, or 'bothy'. The Association maintains more than 100 bothies all over the country and this site gives details of where the huts are and how many people they can accommodate, together with membership details and updates on the status of individual bothies. This is a useful site for any walker or mountaineer exploring Scotland.

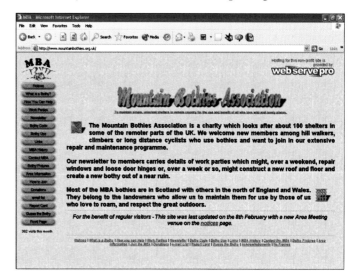

Alpine Clubs

Information on high-level walking in beautiful scenery and on good tracks is available through the Alpine Clubs Web sites.

The highest mountains close to Britain are, of course, the Alps, where the trails are clearly marked and the walker is well looked after. All the Alpine countries have clubs that maintain a network of mountain huts, full lists of which can be found on the clubs' Web sites. Not all the clubs cater properly for the English-language-only browser but, if you are planning a walking holiday, you should be able to get a good idea of where to go and what is available. Some useful practical advice and an accommodation guide is provided by the French Club Alpin site (www.clubalpin.com/fr), although the detailed information is in French. To translate this, you could make use of AltaVista's online translation program by clicking on the Translate link on their home page (www.altavista.co.uk). Paste in the text that you would like translated, select the language pair and a rough translation will be generated.

Italy's Alpine Club – the Club Alpino Italiano (www.cai.it) supplies a guide to the refuges of the Italian mountains, as well as information on excursions and, of course, sports. In addition, Austria's Alpine Club (www.alpenverein.at), its German equivalent (www.alpenverein.de) and the Swiss mountain association (www.bergtourismus.ch/e/huetten.cfm) also offer a good list of huts.

The Swiss (above) and German (left) sites of the Alpine Clubs provide useful information about where to stay for the night when on a walking or hiking holiday, although they don't always cater for English speakers.

Royalty

Queen Elizabeth II has a dignified official Web site, but there are plenty with a more 'common touch'. Whatever you want to know – from corgis to calendars – it's available on the Web.

It seems that we just can't get enough of kings and queens, their children and their extended families. Whether it's in daily newspapers, glossy magazines, on television or at the cinema, you can be sure there will always be a very generous helping of royalty in all its guises. As whatever is represented in the media is inevitably present in depth on the Internet, it shouldn't be surprising to find that there are hundreds of royalty Web sites, many of which combine regal presentation with very good levels of information.

● History made real
People with interests in royalty will approach the subject in different ways – some may prefer to know the details of today's monarchy, others prefer a more historical approach, such as simply learning about the past kings and queens of England, or gaining an understanding of Henry VII's European trade policy, for example.

There's plenty of this sort of information on the Net, ranging from sites that list all the kings and queens, to those that focus on individual monarchs or make available rich collections of original historical source material (see Internet Modern History Sourcebook, page 152). On the latter you'll find significant speeches and statements, which are not just of general interest but are very useful for students of history.

The quality of the content varies from site to site so you do need to look around. Some sites, for example, offer little more than transcripts from a couple of pages of an existing history text book.

● Modern monarchy
The role of the modern monarchy has increasingly been the subject of serious study and examination. As its very existence and purpose are questioned by would-be republicans, the monarchy has joined the ranks of

The Internet is truly the people's communications network – and provides ready access to information about crowned heads of state all over the world.

organizations explaining themselves on the Internet. The official British Monarchy site (see page 151) presents the monarchy in a multi-faceted way, with plenty of interesting and surprising information.

The Prince of Wales, too, has his own official Web presence (see page 151), and this site even has an element of interaction in the shape of forums, where you can contribute to ongoing debates on current topics.

● Royalty around the world
Plenty of other royal families are represented on the Web. A quick surf serves to remind us that the British Royal Family is not the only surviving royal dynasty. More than half a dozen EC countries have a monarch as their head of state, and most of these have an official Web site too.

Monarchies from much further afield, such as those in Thailand and Polynesia, in addition to defunct dynasties, such as the Habsburgs, also

DIANA, PRINCESS OF WALES

You can't really discuss royalty on the Web without mentioning its most famous representative of recent times. Since Diana's death, memorials of all sorts have been created and the Internet is no exception; Yahoo lists more than 100 sites for Diana Memorials alone – and that's restricted to the UK. The majority of these sites are created and maintained by individuals. They vary in their approach, however, and while most are tasteful, some tend to the bizarre. Perhaps the most stylish and appropriately restrained is the elegant site for Althorp, where Diana is buried (www.althorp.com). The site gives a history of the house and visitor information, and there's a good 'virtual tour' for the armchair visitor.

have sites, often with a very high standard of presentation and information, and some of them are featured on these pages.

● Less formal royal sites

As for the second kind of approach to royalty, who could study, say, the reign of Henry VIII without touching on the more personal side of a royal's life? Most of the unofficial royalty Web sites provide a lot of coverage on the relationships – official or otherwise – of the royals. In addition, there are many personal sites run by dedicated amateur 'royal watchers'.

If you want gossip on the royals, you'll find it easily on the Internet, but look a little further afield and you'll find all manner of information on royalty that is likely to prove a lot more rewarding. As a general rule, you will find the best information and presentation from the official or historical sites – but these aren't the best places if you're after scandal.

Royals on the Web

The public and private lives of monarchs and other royals, past and present, can be found on the Internet.

The British Monarchy

www.royal.gov.uk

This is the official Web site of the British Monarchy. As you'd expect, it has a certain dignity, together with a sparse and elegant design. Its aim is partly to perform a PR function, countering the damaging publicity of recent years by providing a clear presentation of what the monarchy is. It covers the monarchy's modern role and what its various members do on a day-to-day basis, but there's also plenty of fun and instruction to be had from this site.

There are good sections on the various palaces and on the Royal Collection of works of art and antiques, together with a brief survey of the monarchy through the ages. There's a Diana page and a visitors' book that you can sign, plus some good links to related sites.

The site also includes an online news magazine in which you can read reports on the latest Royal engagements and take a look at behind-the-scenes activity in the Buckingham Palace press office. You can also post questions, browse the picture gallery, and test your knowledge of Royal media milestones in the online quiz.

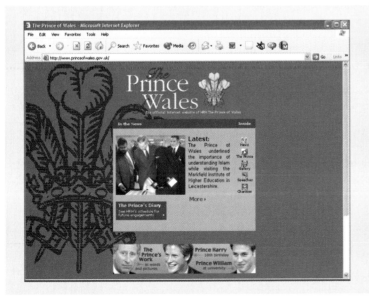

The Official Internet Website of HRH The Prince of Wales

www.princeofwales.gov.uk

This site gives an overview of the busy life and public commitments of the Prince of Wales. You can check his diary to see where he's going and what he's doing over the following month; consult an archive of his speeches and articles; check out the picture gallery of official visits; and see what is happening with his two major charities, the Prince's Trust and the Prince's Youth Business Trust. There are also separate sections on both of the Prince of Wales' sons, Prince William and Prince Harry, which include interviews with the two young princes, as well as links to related sites.

Internet Modern History Sourcebook

www.fordham.edu/halsall/mod/modsbook.html

This is not, strictly speaking, a royalty site. It is instead a collection of source documents, or links to them, which will help those studying or interested in history. There are book excerpts, proclamations, laws, speeches and letters from all sorts of significant historical figures including, of course, a fair number of royals and their associates. For example, you can read a letter from Anne Boleyn to Henry VIII, written in the Tower, pleading her innocence of adultery. Perhaps the highlight though is an excellent collection of speeches by Elizabeth I, which gives a very vivid flavour of her personality and times. There's a wealth of fascinating material on this site – and not just about royalty, of course.

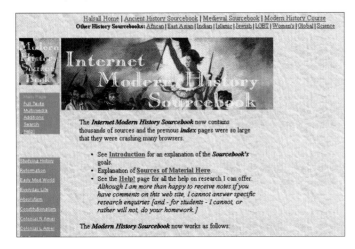

Heraldica

www.heraldica.org

Part of the Heraldica site is an FAQ page on the British Royal Family, (www.heraldica.org/faqs/britfaq.html). The very detailed answers to more than 50 commonly asked questions about the British monarchy could clear up any queries that have been puzzling you. Some of the questions are very specific, for example, 'Was Prince Philip of Greece and Denmark a British subject before he became naturalized in 1947?'

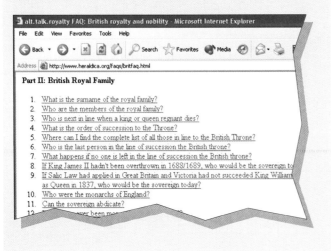

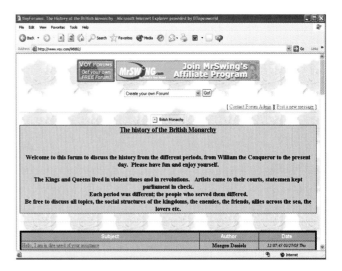

Voy.com

www.voy.com/98082/

This forum-style Web site covers every aspect of the British monarchy, with users posting and responding to questions on both historical and modern issues. Whether you'd like to know more about Queen Elizabeth II or William the Conqueror, this could be the place to try.

The users come from all over the world and have discussed most of the concerns you can think of – including the current state of the monarchy and the question of its future. Besides this exchange of information, people also use the site to advertise the sale of memorabilia and books.

Royal Insight

www.royalinsight.gov.uk

This site is the British Royal Family's very own in-house webzine (online magazine) and is an offshoot of the official Web site of the British Monarchy (see page 151). It isn't as formal, however, and focuses more on the recent engagements of members of the Royal family and the tasks of the press office, than the Monarchy's role and history. It has all the components you would expect to find in a glossy promotional magazine, with good photographs and in-depth features on the current work of the Royals.

The Imperial Family of Japan

www.geocities.com/Tokyo/Temple/3953/

This is not an official site but is nonetheless respectful and authoritative, containing pretty much all you could want to know about Japan's Imperial Family. There are biographies of the Emperor and his family, genealogies, a glossary of titles and functions – and even constitutional documents demonstrating the changing role and power of the Emperor. It has few pictures but lots of information.

The Habsburg Dynasty

www.geocities.com/Vienna/1605/habsburg.htm

The Habsburgs formed a famous royal dynasty that existed for centuries, but ended with the First World War. They might no longer rule, but this site will provide you with a potted history of their heritage, beginning with their rise to power in 1278, through to the diminution of the Austrian Republic by the end of the First World War. There is also a link to view an archive of historical documents of the Austro-Hungarian Empire.

HM the King of Thailand

kanchanapisek.or.th/index.en.html

If you've ever been to Thailand, you'll be aware of the great respect the people have for the monarchy and its current head, King Bhumibol. This neatly designed and illustrated site, created to celebrate the King's Golden Jubilee in 1996, gives a pretty good idea of why. There is detailed information on the many and various projects initiated by the king over the past 50 years, and there's a fascinating section on 'Royal Talents', where we discover that the king is not only a talented jazz musician but also a respected composer of classical Thai music. This is a truly intriguing site.

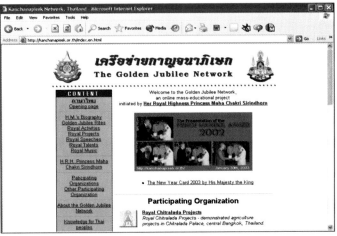

Genealogy

Heredity is intrinsic to the monarchy, and this site aims to fulfil our curiosity about the many dynastic marriages and alliances.

A royal family's genealogy is of interest to many, either for historical reasons, or because they want to find out if they're related and where they stand in line to the throne. There are many royal genealogy sites on the Web. The top site is the Directory of Royal Genealogical Data (www.dcs.hull.ac.uk/public/genealogy/royal/), maintained by Professor Brian Tompsett at the University of Hull. This massive work isn't just a genealogical database of the British Royal Family, it also features 'the genealogy of almost every ruling house in the Western world because of the intermarriage that took place between them at some time or another'. There are some 30,000 names in the database.

Another genealogical site of interest is Descendants of Charlemagne (www8.informatik.uni-erlangen.de/html/chl-enter.html), a very clear presentation of the dynasty founded by the great king. Also fascinating is Genealogical Gleanings (http://uqconnect.net/~zzhsoszy/), which covers the royal families of dozens of African and Asian countries.

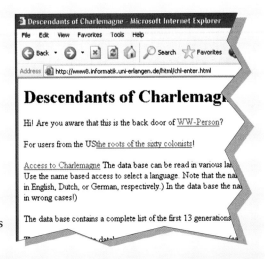

Motorcycling

Motorcycling is big on the Web. There's something for everyone, from sites on classic bikes to online magazines.

Unlike straightforward four-wheel driving, motorcycling retains a certain glamour and excitement, with its image of a man or woman, encased in shiny helmet and leathers, braving the road and the elements on a heroic journey atop a powerful, two-wheeled speed machine. As well as this romantic aspect to motorcycling, there's also a very practical side to this topic, since there's a lot more you can do with a bike, in terms of maintenance and tuning, compared with the options available on a family saloon car.

Many motorcycling sites focus on one or the other of these two aspects of biking. There are the glamour sites, featuring what might be called the *Easy Rider* aspects of biking – touring exotic regions of the world, or racing a 1000cc monster at over 240km/h. Then the gritty, practical sites help you to find that missing grommet for your vintage Norton or give life-saving tips on wet-weather riding. Some sites do cater for fans of both glamour and grit.

Whatever their content, the number and quality of Web outlets for biking have increased greatly. In particular, sites forming motorcycle webzines such as www.motorcycle.com and www.motorcycle-uk.com (see opposite) supply a wide range of well-written and attractively designed content. These two sites, and others like them, are probably the best places to start if you have no specific purpose in mind: you're bound to find several articles to interest you.

● Machine makers

The manufacturers, too, have finally decided to take the Web seriously (see page 156). They all now have extremely stylish sites which act principally as online brochures, with exciting pictures and the enticing specifications of their sexier models.

Zip up your leathers, pull on your helmet and fire up your browser – it's time to ride into the Webscape to check out the range of sites devoted to motorcycling.

Some are getting more interactive, offering you the chance to insure online, find a dealer, view the various colour options or buy a bike.

● Two-wheeled friends

As anyone driving around the countryside on a fine afternoon will have noticed, bikers exhibit a very high level of camaraderie. This tendency is well served on the Web in the form of forums, chat rooms and newsgroups, and also by a thriving, online classified sales culture; many sites give you the chance to buy or sell anything from a massive Honda Gold Wing touring bike to a spare left gauntlet.

There is also, of course, a great nostalgic interest among bikers for the classic bikes of yesteryear. A thriving section of the motorcycling community devotes its time to restoring, riding and talking about classic bikes – and they're only too happy to show us the pictures and give us the story on the Web. Those who don't want to tinker can simply admire the stunning machines at the online classic bike museums and dream of owning them.

SITES FOR CLASSIC MOTORCYCLING

A significant number of sites are devoted to the passion for classic motorcycles. The enthusiasts' magazine *Classic Motorcycle* has its own site (www.classicmotorcycle.co.uk), which contains classified ads and an online shop although there's little of the content that you find in the magazine.

At www.oldbikemart.co.uk you'll find a classified section that's extremely well stocked with bikes; it's just the place to look if you're in the market for, say, a 1920 Excelsior 1000cc vee twin. The links section of the same site is one of the best places to search for more specialized sites.

As one would expect, classic bikes often need work, either as restoration or repair. Classic Bike Parts (www.classicbikeparts.co.uk) is probably the best place to start looking for parts and information. You need to join up to use features such as Technical help, but there are still good public sections, such as the Parts Index.

Sites for motorcycle fans

There's both powerful sports machines and down-to-earth advice waiting on the Web.

Motorcycle Online

www.motorcycle.com

This is the home of one of the oldest, but still one of the best, biking webzines around. Even though it tends to be American orientated, bikers from anywhere will find plenty to entertain and inform them here. On the consumer side there are exhaustive product and accessory reviews, together with dozens of authoritative bike road tests. In the Multimedia Archive you'll find loads of photos, videos and audioclips relating to biking, while the Virtual Museum contains plenty of detail on 'vintage iron' and a link to the Guggenheim Museum's Art of the Motorcycle exhibition. In common with many special-interest Web sites, there's a thriving forum for sharing anecdotes and road stories, and a classified section for buying and selling parts and bikes. Whether you want basic knowledge or more advanced biking information, this classic site is well worth a visit.

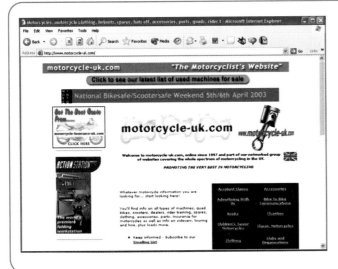

Motorcycle UK

www.motorcycle-uk.com

Half webzine, half motorcycle Web mall, this site has something for everyone. Content is either exclusive to the site itself or generated through links to smaller, specialized sites, as with custom parts (www.custom-wizard.com) or a searchable dealer database (www.motorcycledealer.co.uk).

You'll also find sections on the racing scene, clubs and organizations and a good classified section with all sorts of bikes and accessories for sale. In addition, there are links to sections on roadside first aid, legal advice, how to prevent your bike from being stolen and much more. All in all, this site is a very handy resource for motorcyclists in the UK and if the site itself doesn't have what you need, it'll probably have a link to one that does.

BikeSafe

www.bikesafe.co.uk

Motorcycling has a high accident and fatality rate, so any initiative to promote safer riding is welcome. This admirable site is a collaborative effort between a number of UK police forces and other organizations. There's lots of good advice and information on staying safe on a bike, covering issues such as the right kind of tyres to fit, riding safely in groups, protective clothing and first aid.

The site also deals with the techniques of defensive riding, where anticipation, observation and caution are paramount. There is much encouragement for riders to seek further training as this has been statistically proven to reduce the chances of having an accident. This is a site that all bikers who are concerned with good riding and staying safe should endeavour to check out.

Bike manufacturers

Only a few years ago the bike makers pretty much ignored the Web. Now they've roared in with sites that are both stylish and practical.

BIKE MANUFACTURERS' sites contain more than lists of models and dealers. The sites shown here display useful information about the products as well as a variety of features likely to be of interest to potential customers. The Suzuki Web site, for example, includes details of the company's sporting achievements while Ducati's site offers a chat facility. The sites also reflect the philosophy and reputation of the companies: Ducati's site is a thing of beauty whereas Harley-Davidson places the emphasis on its biker stance.

At the neat, informative Honda site (www.honda.co.uk), you can order a brochure, find a dealer and buy bike insurance. The details of each model are clearly set out.

Suzuki's site (www.suzuki.co.uk) contains information on model and dealer details, motocross and racing, and even has a section on their sporting achievements.

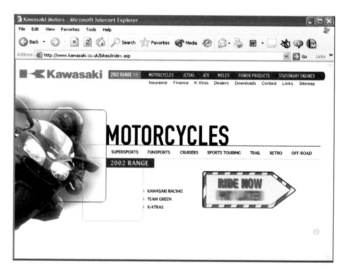

The Kawasaki site (www.kawasaki.co.uk) is one of the less stylish sites, but it has a broad content similar to that offered by Suzuki.

Ducati's site (www.ducati.com) is suave and stylish. It also boasts a photo gallery, online shopping and a chance to chat with famous racers, engineers and designers.

Harley's site (www.harley-davidson.com) aims to give you a taste of the Harley 'experience' and emphasizes its own brand of biker philosophy.

visordown

www.visordown.com

Motorcyclists are a friendly bunch, and you can see just how much they like to swap stories and items of biker lore by the number of postings in this very popular site hosting a variety of forums. There are more than 13,000 postings in the Gallery section alone. In fact, there are forums here for every aspect of motorcycling you could possibly imagine, where you will find a huge collection of matters under discussion, ranging from survival skills to bikers' pubs. The whole site is neatly designed and easy to navigate, so whether you want to participate in the ongoing threads of discussion or just enjoy the thoughts and advice of the thousands of other users, you should check it out.

Classic Racing Motorcycle Club

www.crmc.co.uk

This simple and fairly basic site is dedicated to preserving, using and racing classic motorcycles (motorcycles manufactured between 1945 and 1972), although post-Classic machines (motorcycles manufactured before 1981) are also raced. This site is aimed at members of the club who participate in and/or watch races, but it will also be of interest to non-members who are motorcycle fanatics. There is a forum (which you needn't be a member to use) where people exchange advice and bike parts, as well as 'Items wanted' and 'Items for sale' sections. In addition, there are photos from previous races and an extensive list of links to other motorcycle-based Web sites.

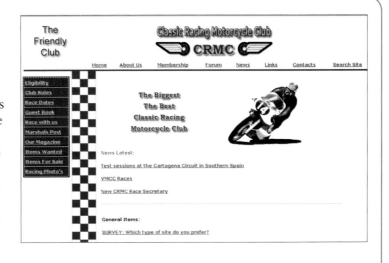

The Allen Vintage Motorcycle Museum

www.allenmuseum.com

Just outside Boston, Massachusetts, this architect-designed, purpose-built museum is full of gorgeous vintage motorcycles. The museum contains a range of bikes from 1955 to the present day; it even boasts that it has a replica of a 1950s British motorcycle shop plus a wide range of memorabilia.

Unfortunately, you can't visit the museum itself as it is private, but the curators have chosen an interesting range of bikes for the virtual offering, which is divided into racing motorcycles, road bikes and custom replica motorcycles. Each entry is accompanied by a photograph.

● **About the index**
Text in italics is used for cross-references within the index (as in *see also...*). Page numbers in bold type denote the main entries for a topic.

● **Acknowledgments**
Abbreviations: t = top; b = bottom;
r = right; l = left; c = centre;
bkg = background. All cartoons
are by Chris Bramley

8t	Lyndon Parker/De Agostini
12tr	Lyndon Parker/De Agostini
14	Lyndon Parker/De Agostini
16	The Stock Market
18	Tony Stone Images
19br	International Business Machines
22	Lyndon Parker/De Agostini
23tr	Lyndon Parker/De Agostini
24	Lyndon Parker/De Agostini
32tr	Science Photo Library/ Mehau Kulyk
34	Lyndon Parker/De Agostini
36tr	Tony Stone Images/Brendon Beirne
38	Lyndon Parker/De Agostini
42tr	Tony Stone Images
44tr	Lyndon Parker/De Agostini
48	Lyndon Parker/De Agostini

50	Lyndon Parker/De Agostini
52	The Stock Market
56	International Business Machines
58	Tony Stone Images
62b	Lyndon Parker/DeAgostini
64	Microsoft Corporation
68tr	Lyndon Parker/De Agostini
70	Lyndon Parker/De Agostini
74	The Stock Market
78	Images Colour Library
82	Lyndon Parker/De Agostini
86	Lyndon Parker/De Agostini
90	Lyndon Parker/De Agostini
92b	Lyndon Parker/De Agostini
96	Lyndon Parker/De Agostini
98	Lyndon Parker/De Agostini
99	Lyndon Parker/De Agostini
100	Intel
101tl	David Parker/Seagate Microelectronics Ltd/SPL
101br	Rosenfeld Images Ltd/SPL
102	Tony Stone Images
103	Photonica/Neal Farris
104	Lyndon Parker/De Agostini

105b	Lyndon Parker/De Agostini
106tr	Xircom
107t,b	Xircom
108tr	The Stock Market
108c	International Business Machines
108bl	Toshiba American Information Systems Inc
109(all)	Mesh Computers PLC
110	Palm Inc
114	Tony Stone Images/Tim Brown/ Olney Vasan
115t	Nokia
115b	Handspring Inc
116	The Stock Market
118tr	Lyndon Parker/De Agostini
120bl	Lyndon Parker/De Agostini
130tr	Zefa/The Stock Market
132tr	Stephen Bartholomew/De Agostini
134	Lyndon Parker/De Agostini
138	Lyndon Parker/De Agostini
142	The Stock Market
146	Tony Stone Images
150	Tony Stone Images
154	The Stock Market